Rachel's
ood for Living

2

Rachel's
Food for Living
RACHEL ALLEN

Collins

Dedication

I dedicate this book to my Grandmother, Sheila O'Neill, and my Grandfather, Hans Reichenfeld, with love.

Contents

Introduction ❁ 8

Food for the Soul ❁ 10
Childhood Favourites ❁ 36
Making Memories ❁ 58
Something to Celebrate ❁ 80
The Lazy Sunday ❁ 100
An Elegant Afternoon ❁ 122
Pleasure Without the Guilt ❁ 142
Food for Romance ❁ 164
For the Love of Chocolate ❁ 188
Classic Dishes ❁ 206

Index ❁ 236
Acknowledgements ❁ 240

Introduction

Food has the amazing potential to be comforting, uplifting, restorative, nurturing, energising and many other things besides. It plays a hugely significant role in our personal lives, both physically and emotionally and can lift us up when we are low and keep us up when we are on top of the world. Eating can be steeped in ritual or be utterly spontaneous but one thing is for certain – the feelings that food stirs go far beyond mere biology.

I love the way that certain aromas and flavours can instantly conjure up vivid memories. They send us back to our childhood kitchens, tugging at our grandmothers' apron strings, or to other times and places in our lives that hold special significance. For me it is the smell of roast stuffed chicken and potatoes that fills me with joyful recollections of my mother's incredible Sunday dinners.

Food makes the best gift, whether it's hot buttered toast for someone with the blues or an elaborate three-course romantic feast for the one you love. The time we take to lovingly prepare a meal can pay dividends in the way it makes others feel cared for.

Even the simplest foods are enough to inspire a happy social occasion. One of my greatest pleasures is catching up with girlfriends over tea and sympathy (and a big pile of biscuits!). We all know that, 'Come round for a cuppa' really means, 'Come round and let's chat for hours and laugh until it hurts.'

This book is filled with foods that have special meaning for me or for my family and friends. I hope that these recipes will make for fun and memorable cooking and eating for you, too!

p.s. The oven temperatures in this book are for a conventional oven, but if I am using a fan oven, then I usually reduce the temperature by 10 per cent.

Rachel's
food for
Living

Food for the Soul

There are times when we all need a bit of comfort in a bowl. These are the times when you want food that makes you feel as though you're wrapped up in a blanket, food that gives you a warm and cosy feeling, food that restores both mentally and physically. Each of us has our own comfort foods. For some, this might be as simple as tea and toast, for others it might be more substantial, such as a big meaty stew eaten while curled up on the sofa. Whatever they are, they're sure to make you feel safe and nurtured. This chapter includes some of my favourite foods to beat the blues!

Spanish Chorizo and Chickpea Soup

SERVES 4–6

1 tbsp olive oil
125g (5oz) chorizo, diced
1 onion, peeled and
    finely chopped
2 celery stalks, finely chopped
2 cloves of garlic, peeled
    and crushed or grated
1 x 400g tin of chickpeas,
    undrained
2 x 400g tins of chopped
    tomatoes (or 8 fresh ripe
    tomatoes, peeled and
    chopped)
1 litre (1¾ pints) chicken stock
Salt and freshly ground
    black pepper
250g (9oz) spinach, destalked
    and finely chopped, or baby
    spinach leaves left whole

This is such a soothing soup on a rainy day, and the flavours always remind me of sunnier summer days. It's a substantial soup, but not too heavy – perfect for a meal in itself. This soup reheats well, in fact the flavours even improve. And of course you don't need to use imported chorizo – there are many wonderful locally produced versions which are equally delicious.

1 Place the olive oil in a large saucepan on the heat and add the diced chorizo. Cook for 1–2 minutes until the chorizo releases its oils, then add the chopped onion, celery and garlic. Cook on a gentle heat with the lid on until the onion is completely cooked, about 10 minutes, then remove the lid and turn up the heat and cook for a minute to slightly brown the onion.
2 Add the chickpeas and their liquid, chopped tomatoes and the stock. Season with salt and pepper and bring up to the boil. Simmer for about 20 minutes until the tomatoes are soft and the chickpeas have absorbed all the flavours. Taste for seasoning, adding more salt and pepper if necessary.
3 While the mixture is still simmering, add the spinach and cook for 1 minute, until the spinach is soft. Serve in big, warm bowls.

Leek, Potato and Blue Cheese Soup

I love this soup – it's rich, smooth and velvety. This makes a lovely meal on its own with some crusty bread on the side, or serve as a starter for a wintery dinner party.

———————— · ❧ · ————————

1 Melt the butter in a medium-sized saucepan, add the leeks, potatoes and bay leaves. Season with salt and pepper and cover. Turn the heat down to low and let the vegetables sweat for 10 minutes, stirring every now and then to ensure they don't burn (see also the handy tip below).

2 After 10 minutes add the stock, increase the heat and simmer for a further 8–10 minutes until the potatoes and leeks are soft. Remove the bay leaves, add the cream and the crumbled blue cheese and transfer to a liquidiser. Whiz the soup until it is smooth and velvety. Return to the saucepan to re-heat, tasting and seasoning if necessary.

3 To serve, pour the soup into warm bowls and sprinkle with the extra crumbled blue cheese.

Rachel's handy tips ❧

❧ If making this soup with a strong blue cheese like Roquefort or Gorgonzola, I only add 100g (4oz), but if you are using a milder blue cheese like Cashel Blue, you might need 125–150g (4¹/2–5oz).

❧ When sweating onions or other vegetables for a long time, I like to cover them with a butter wrapper or a piece of greaseproof paper as well as the saucepan lid. This helps to retain the moisture and makes sure they don't burn.

SERVES 4–6
VEGETARIAN
25g (1oz) butter
2 leeks (about 300g/12oz), dark green tops removed, white bits thinly sliced
2 potatoes (about 175g/6oz), peeled and chopped
2 bay leaves
Salt and freshly ground black pepper
1 litre (1³/4 pints) light vegetable or chicken stock
75ml (2¹/2fl oz) single cream
100–150g (4–5oz) blue cheese, such as Cashel Blue, Stilton, Gorgonzola or Roquefort, crumbled (see handy tip), plus 25g (1oz) for serving

Italian Baked Pancakes with Cheese and Tomato

SERVES 4–6
VEGETARIAN

FOR THE PANCAKE BATTER
(MAKES 8)
125g (5oz) flour
Pinch of salt
2 eggs
125ml (4fl oz) milk
125ml (4fl oz) water
15g (½oz) butter, melted
Sunflower oil, for oiling
   the frying pan

FOR THE TOMATO SAUCE
3 tbsp olive oil
1 onion, peeled and finely
   sliced
4 cloves of garlic, peeled
   and crushed or grated
Salt, freshly ground black
   pepper and sugar
2 x 400g tins of chopped
   tomatoes or 900g (2lb)
   fresh tomatoes, peeled
   and chopped
3 tbsp torn fresh basil leaves

FOR THE FILLING
300g (11oz) fresh mozzarella,
   grated
100g (4oz) ricotta
25g (1oz) Parmesan cheese,
   finely grated, plus a bit
   extra for sprinkling

This recipe was inspired by a conversation I had with the great Italian chef Aldo Zilli. He told me a wonderful story about his mother using light pancakes as an alternative to pasta in certain dishes, and I've discovered they work wonderfully with rich tomato sauces. This recipe uses the pancakes in place of lasagne sheets, which adds a fluffiness to the dish. I love the way it comes out of the oven, sizzling and bubbling to the table. It's a perfect family dinner.

———————— · ❧ · ————————

1 First make the pancakes. Place the flour and salt in a bowl. Make a well in the centre and drop in the eggs. Start to whisk, gradually add in the milk and water, whisking all the time, until the batter is smooth and free of lumps. Add in the melted butter and set aside. The batter can sit like this in the fridge for 24 hours.

2 Next make the tomato sauce. Place the olive oil in a wide saucepan, add the onion and garlic, season with salt and pepper, then cover and cook on a low heat until the onions are completely soft. Add the tomatoes and half the basil, leave uncovered and cook for about 20 minutes until the tomatoes are soft and the sauce has thickened. Add the remaining herbs and season to taste with salt, pepper and a pinch of sugar.

3 While the tomato sauce is cooking, you can make the pancakes. Place a medium-sized frying pan on a high heat and allow to become very hot. Pour the batter into a jug for easy pouring. Wipe the frying pan with an oiled piece of kitchen paper. Pour in just enough batter to cover the base of the pan – it will start to cook as soon as it hits the pan so swirl it around the base immediately.

4 Cook on a high heat for 30 seconds–1 minute until the pancake is golden brown around the edge. Using a fish slice or palette knife, carefully but quickly flip the pancake over (you might need to take the pan off the heat while you do this) and cook the other side for another 30 seconds–1 minute until golden brown. Remove to a plate and cook the remaining pancakes in the same way. You will need a total of eight pancakes.

5 Preheat the oven to 180°C (350°F), Gas mark 4.

6 Mix the cheeses together in a bowl, to make a spreadable paste.

7 To assemble the dish, place a pancake on the bottom of a 25cm (10in) square or round ovenproof dish, spread with a thin layer of the cheese mixture, top with another pancake and continue assembling, alternative seven layers of pancake and filling. Finish with a top layer of pancake. Pour the tomato sauce over the top, sprinkle with the remaining 25g (1oz) grated Parmesan.

8 Place in the oven (though it can also be stored in the fridge overnight or frozen at this stage). Bake for 30–40 minutes until the sauce is bubbling around the edges and the centre feels hot when a skewer is inserted. Take out of the oven, cut into wedges and serve with a lovely green salad.

Rigatoni with Courgettes, Lemon and Basil

This is one of my all-time favourite comfort foods. It's surprisingly refreshing for a pasta dish due to the fresh flavours of the lemon, courgette and basil, but the mascarpone and cream cheese are warmly satisfying.

SERVES 4
VEGETARIAN

450g (1lb) rigatoni or other pasta shapes
2 tbsp olive oil
4 small or 2 medium courgettes, halved lengthways, seeds removed and thinly sliced at an angle
100g (4oz) mascarpone cheese or soft cream cheese
3 tbsp milk
Finely grated zest of ½ lemon
3 tbsp torn or sliced fresh basil
Salt and freshly ground black pepper

1 Bring a large pot of water to the boil with a good pinch of salt, then cook the pasta according to the packet's instructions.

2 While the pasta is cooking, heat the olive oil in a medium-sized frying pan over a high heat, then add the courgettes. Cook for 3–4 minutes until just softened and lightly golden. In a bowl, mix together the cheese, milk, lemon zest and 1 tablespoon of the basil. Add to the courgettes in the pan and toss together on the heat for 1 minute, until the cheese has melted. Season to taste.

3 Drain the pasta and return to the large pot. Add the creamy courgettes and gently stir to mix. Then pour into a warm serving bowl and scatter with the remaining basil. Serve immediately.

Rachel's handy tip

If the courgettes are 12cm (4½in) or smaller, there is no need to halve them lengthways or remove the seeds. Just remove the ends and slice thinly.

Creamy Coconut Prawns with Spiced Banana Raita

SERVES 4

FOR THE PANCH PURAN
1 tsp brown mustard seeds
1 tsp whole nigella seeds
1 tsp ground fenugreek seeds
1 tsp ground fennel seeds
1 tsp ground cumin seeds
2 tsp turmeric powder
1 level tsp salt

FOR SPICED BANANA RAITA
400ml (14fl oz) natural yoghurt
1/2–1 tbsp Garam Masala spice
2 good handfuls of raisins
   (optional), soaked in boiling
   water for 10 minutes, then
   drained
2 tbsp freshly chopped mint
1 banana, very thinly sliced
Juice and zest of 1/2 lime

FOR THE COCONUT PRAWNS
4 tsp mustard oil (or sunflower
   or corn oil)
1kg (2lb 4oz) peeled tiger
   prawns
1 tbsp butter, clarified butter
   or vegetable oil
1 heaped tbsp gram flour
   (or 1 tbsp of plain flour)
1 x 400ml tin coconut milk
1 generous tbsp tamarind
   paste mixed with 2 tbsp hot
   water till mushy, then
   pushed through a sieve to
   get rid of the stones
1 chilli, deseeded and diced
450ml (16fl oz) fish stock or
   water
Salt, to taste
Handful of fresh coriander,
   chopped

This is an absolutely divine Bengalese recipe, given to me by a friend, Arun Kapil, who imports spices from his family in India. Seafood is central to the region's cuisine – every day the locals catch the freshest fish and the plumpest prawns in the Bay of Bengal and typically combine them with tamarind, mild spices and coconut, according to traditional family recipes. Here, Arun has devised this deliciously simple recipe combining prawns, creamy coconut milk, exotic tamarind and an Indian spice blend, panch puran.

1 To make the panch puran spice blend, mix together all of the ingredients in a small bowl.

2 Then, in a medium-sized bowl, mix the mustard oil and 1 teaspoon of the spice blend. Add the tiger prawns, mix well and set aside for 30 minutes.

3 Make the raita by mixing the ingredients in a medium bowl. Add seasoning to taste and keep to one side.

4 In a large, heavy-bottomed frying pan or wok, heat the clarified butter or oil to smoking point and add the rest of the dry spice blend. Reduce the heat and toast for 10–15 seconds, constantly stirring. Add the flour and stir or whisk until smooth (this should only take about 2 minutes). Don't worry how it looks at this stage – you're making a kind of roux and it's supposed to be a dry(ish) paste.

5 Add the coconut milk, tamarind paste, diced chilli and a good pinch of salt, and keep stirring or whisking until it's smooth (another couple of minutes). Add the water or fish stock bit by bit until it's the thickness of double cream.

6 Add the prawns, turn up the heat and bring rapidly to the boil. Turn the heat back down and simmer for only 1 minute until the prawns are just cooked; any longer and they become rubbery.

7 Turn off the heat, add the coriander and a squeeze of lime juice and season to taste. Serve immediately with plenty of basmati rice and the raita.

Rachel's handy tips

You can buy panch puran ready-made from many Asian
shops or big supermarkets if you're short on time. You can
also serve this with the Yoghurt and Cucumber Raita on
page 119; use half the quantity.

Pasta with Roasted Peppers and Mozzarella

Sometimes the simplest recipes make the best pick-me-ups. This is such a quick and easy meal, and you can just close your eyes and dream of the Tuscan hills. If you keep roasted peppers in the fridge, it's all the faster to make!

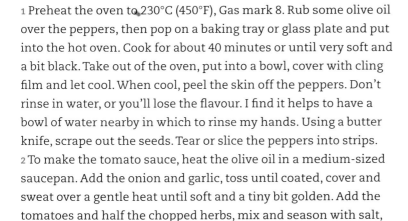

1 Preheat the oven to 230°C (450°F), Gas mark 8. Rub some olive oil over the peppers, then pop on a baking tray or glass plate and put into the hot oven. Cook for about 40 minutes or until very soft and a bit black. Take out of the oven, put into a bowl, cover with cling film and let cool. When cool, peel the skin off the peppers. Don't rinse in water, or you'll lose the flavour. I find it helps to have a bowl of water nearby in which to rinse my hands. Using a butter knife, scrape out the seeds. Tear or slice the peppers into strips.

2 To make the tomato sauce, heat the olive oil in a medium-sized saucepan. Add the onion and garlic, toss until coated, cover and sweat over a gentle heat until soft and a tiny bit golden. Add the tomatoes and half the chopped herbs, mix and season with salt, pepper and a pinch of sugar. Gently simmer, uncovered, for approximately 30 minutes or until softened. Add the remaining chopped herbs at the end.

3 Cook the pasta in a large pot of salted boiling water until just cooked, then drain and toss with the tomato sauce, add the roast peppers and mozzarella, season to taste and serve.

SERVES 4–6
VEGETARIAN

FOR THE ROAST PEPPERS
Olive oil
2 peppers, choose from red, yellow or orange (green peppers can be bitter)

FOR THE TOMATO SAUCE
3 tbsp olive oil
1 onion, peeled and sliced
1 clove of garlic, peeled and crushed
1 x 400g tin chopped tomatoes (or 450g/1lb tomatoes, peeled and chopped)
2 tbsp chopped herbs, such as basil, parsley, marjoram or tarragon
Salt, freshly ground black pepper and sugar

TO SERVE
450g (1lb) dried pasta, such as penne, fusilli or farfalle
1 x 150g (5oz) ball of mozzarella, broken into little pieces of 1cm (1/2in)

Slow-cooked Lamb Shanks with Piperonata

SERVES 4

FOR THE LAMB SHANKS
125g (5oz) streaky bacon, chopped into 1cm (½in) pieces
2 tbsp olive oil
4 lamb shanks
Salt and freshly ground black pepper
1 large onion, peeled and chopped
4 cloves of garlic, peeled and crushed or grated
2 stalks of celery, chopped
2 carrots, peeled and chopped
1 x 400g tin chopped tomatoes
225ml (8fl oz) red wine
225ml (8fl oz) lamb or chicken stock
2 sprigs of fresh rosemary or 4 sprigs of fresh thyme
1 bay leaf
2 strips of orange peel (removed with a peeler)
Caster sugar

FOR THE PIPERONATA
3 tbsp olive oil
1 small onion, peeled and sliced
2 cloves of garlic, peeled and crushed or grated
Salt and freshly ground black pepper
2 small red peppers
1 small yellow pepper
1 x 400g tin of chopped tomatoes or 4 large ripe tomatoes, peeled and sliced
1–2 tsp sugar
2 tbsp torn fresh basil or chopped fresh marjoram

There are times when perfectly cooked lamb seems the cure for just about anything. I love lamb shanks for their tender, succulent texture and sweet, delicious flavour. They're best cooked at a low temperature for a long time, about 3–4 hours, by which time the meat will be falling off the bone. The piperonata is a wonderful pepper and tomato stew that is very versatile. Serve it as a vegetable accompaniment to a roast as here, or with egg dishes such as omelettes. It can be made in advance and frozen. I often serve this dish with mashed potato (see page 27).

1 First prepare the lamb shanks. Preheat the oven to 150°C (300°F), Gas mark 2.
2 Boil the bacon in boiling water in a small saucepan for 1 minute, then rinse in cold water.
3 Place an ovenproof medium–large casserole pot or heavy large saucepan on a medium heat, pour in the olive oil and put in the lamb shanks, season and allow to brown slightly on all sides. Add all the remaining ingredients, season with salt, pepper and a couple of good pinches of sugar.
4 Bring up to the boil, then place in the oven and cook for 3 hours or until very tender – the meat should be almost falling off the bone.
5 While the lamb is cooking, make the piperonata. Heat the olive oil in a medium-sized casserole or saucepan. Add the onion and garlic, season with salt and pepper and cover (see the handy tip on page 15). Allow to cook gently on a low heat until the onion is soft, about 8 minutes.
6 Meanwhile, slice the peppers. Cut the peppers into quarters from top to bottom, remove the stalk and seeds, then cut into short slices crossways or cut into squares about 3cm (1¼in).
7 When the onion is soft, add the peppers, toss to mix, replace the lid and cook for another 8 or so minutes until the peppers are very soft.
8 Add in the tomatoes and season with salt, pepper and sugar. Cook uncovered for 15–20 minutes on a low heat until the sauce has

thickened and all the vegetables are cooked. Add the chopped herbs and season to taste.

9 When the lamb is cooked, take it out of the oven. I like to remove half of the sauce and liquidise it before adding it back into the pot.

10 Season to taste and serve together with the piperonata and mashed potato or bread, or allow to cool and reheat gently the following day.

Rachel's handy tips

❀ To peel fresh tomatoes, cut a cross through the skin, drop them into boiling water for 10–15 seconds, then drain, cool and peel.

❀ I sometimes add chopped chilli and fresh coriander into the piperonata instead of basil or marjoram. If I don't have any fresh herbs to hand, I add a dollop of pesto in at the end, for that lovely basil flavour.

Perfect Mash

Sometimes there is nothing better than plain old mash, even just on its own! Of course, it's delicious with so many foods, best of all with stews or roasts. You can leave it plain, or add buttered cabbage to make traditional Irish Colcannon, or add peas boiled in milk to make Irish Champ. Mash is incredibly versatile and marries well with so many flavours, so experiment with your additions, such as grated cheese, chopped herbs, spices (such as turmeric), crushed garlic, mustard, even horseradish! Mash also makes a great topping for pies and casseroles (see the recipe for Smoked Fish Pie on page 213).

SERVES 4
VEGETARIAN
1kg (2lb 4oz) floury potatoes (new potatoes are too waxy for mashing)
50g (2oz) butter
200ml (7fl oz) boiling milk, or 150ml (¼ pint) boiling milk and 60ml (2fl oz) single cream
Salt and freshly ground black pepper

1 Clean the potatoes, but do not peel them. Place in a saucepan of cold water with a good pinch of salt.

2 Bring the water up to the boil and cook for 10 minutes. Then pour out all but about 4cm (1½in) of the water and continue to cook the potatoes on a very low heat. Do not be tempted to stick a knife into them – the skins will break and they will just break up and get soggy if you do. About 20 minutes later, when you think the potatoes might be cooked, test them with a skewer; if they are soft, take them off the heat. I find that cooking potatoes in their skins is the best way to make fluffy potatoes, ideal for mashing.

3 Peel the potatoes while they are still hot, holding them in a tea towel to prevent scalding your hands. Mash them immediately. Add the butter, but don't add any milk until they are free of lumps. When the potatoes are mashed, add the boiling milk (or milk and cream) – you may not need it all, or you may need more, depending on the texture of the potatoes. Add some salt and pepper to taste.

Rachel's handy tip

If you want to make the mash in advance, add a little extra milk, as the potatoes dry out as they sit. The mash keeps well in a warm oven as long as it is covered with a lid, plate or tin foil.

Pork and Mushroom Pie with Gentle Spices

SERVES 4

FOR THE ROUX
100g (4oz) butter
100g (4oz) plain flour

FOR THE FILLING
25g (1oz) butter
2 onions, peeled and chopped
Salt and freshly ground pepper
1 tsp ground cumin
1 tsp ground coriander
680g (1½lb) pork, cut into
    1–2cm (½–¾in) cubes
    (shoulder or leg, fat removed)
250ml (9fl oz) chicken stock
1 tbsp olive oil
300g (11oz) button mushrooms,
    wiped and sliced or left
    whole or quartered if they
    are small
250ml (9fl oz) single cream
1 tbsp chopped fresh parsley

FOR THE TOPPING
300g (11oz) puff or flaky pastry,
    rolled to 5mm (¼in) thick
1 egg, beaten

OR
1.25kg (2lb 12oz) mashed
    potato (see page 27)

Savoury pies always rank very high on people's lists of soothing foods. This is a great dish to make in advance, giving the aromatic spices even more time to infuse into the meat.

———————— · ✤ · ————————

1 To make the roux, heat a medium-sized saucepan over a medium heat and melt the butter, then add the flour, continuing to stir. Allow it to cook for 2 minutes. Pour into a small bowl and use straight away, or allow to cool and put in the fridge. Preheat the oven to 160°C (325°F), Gas mark 3.

2 Melt the butter in a medium-sized casserole and add the onions and seasoning. Cover and sweat on a low heat for 5 minutes. Turn up the heat, add the ground spices and pork. Toss for a few minutes until the pork changes colour, then add the stock. Cover and cook in the oven for 45–60 minutes or until the pork is tender.

3 While the pork is cooking, heat the olive oil in a pan on a high heat and toss in the mushrooms. Cook for a few minutes until they are pale golden and then add to the pork after 30 minutes.

4 When the pork is cooked, remove the pork and mushrooms from their cooking liquid and set aside in a dish in a warm place. Add the cream to the juices in the pot and boil with the lid off for a few minutes until the flavour strengthens. To thicken the sauce, slowly whisk in about 2 tablespoons of roux while the mixture is boiling. Add the chopped parsley and return the pork and mushrooms. Season to taste and place in individual dishes or a large pie dish.

5 For a pastry topping, preheat the oven to 230°C (450°F), Gas mark 8. For a mashed potato topping, preheat it to 180°C (350°F), Gas mark 4.

6 For a pastry top, cut the pastry to the same size as the top of the pie dish and arrange over the filling. Make a hole in the centre for steam to escape. Brush with the beaten egg to glaze. Cook in the oven for 10 minutes, then turn down the temperature to 190°C (375°F), Gas mark 5 and cook for about 20 minutes, until the pastry is golden brown.

7 For a mashed potato top, arrange the mashed potato on top of the filling and lightly score the surface. Cook in the oven for 30–40 minutes or until golden brown on top and bubbling hot.

Greek Lamb, Onion and Butter Bean Stew

This is a rich and wonderful recipe from my mother-in-law, Darina, that I absolutely adore. We often make it at the cookery school. Like many other stews, it becomes even more delicious if made a day or two in advance. Serve with just a green salad, some mashed or boiled potatoes, or rice.

1 Heat the olive oil in a medium-sized frying pan. Toss the meat, onions and garlic in the hot pan in batches until light golden, then transfer to a medium–large ovenproof casserole.

2 Drain the butter beans and add to the casserole with the bay leaves and thyme. Pour in the stock, to come about halfway up the meat, and add some salt and pepper.

3 Bring to the boil and simmer for 1–1½ hours, either on a low hob or in an oven preheated to 160°C (325°F), Gas mark 3, until all the ingredients are tender and juicy. Taste the stew – it may need more seasoning. Sprinkle with chopped parsley and serve.

Rachel's handy tip

If you are using dried butter beans, soak them in water for 5–6 hours or overnight. Drain and cover with fresh cold water and simmer in a medium-sized saucepan for 35–40 minutes until they are cooked through. Do not add salt because this will toughen the beans' skin.

SERVES 4–6

2 tbsp olive oil
1.1kg (2½lb) shoulder of lamb, cut into 4cm (1½in) cubes
700g (1½lb) baby onions, peeled, or large onions, peeled and cut into quarters
6 cloves of garlic, peeled and chopped
2 x 400g tins of cooked butterbeans, drained, or 225g (8oz) dried butter beans (see the handy tip for cooking instructions)
2 bay leaves
Generous sprig of fresh thyme
450ml (16fl oz) lamb or chicken stock
Salt and freshly ground black pepper
2 tbsp coarsely chopped fresh parsley

Bacon and Sausage Stew with Beans

SERVES 4

75g (3oz) dried black turtle beans (or black-eyed beans)

75g (3oz) borlotti beans or kidney beans

75g (3oz) cannellini beans or haricot beans or 2 x 400g tins of cooked beans, drained

8 rashers smoked bacon (about 300g/11oz), sliced into lardons

2 tbsp olive oil

4 cloves of garlic, peeled and chopped

2 x 400g tins of chopped tomatoes or 800g (1lb 12oz) fresh tomatoes

1.2 litres (2 pints) chicken stock

225g (8oz) cabbage (preferably green, such as Savoy), thinly sliced

300g (11oz) smoked sausage, sliced into 5mm (1/4in) thick pieces

2 tsp chopped fresh thyme

1 tbsp chopped fresh parsley

Salt and freshly ground black pepper

This is simply heaven in a casserole dish! It is a hearty meal, and the perfect reward after a long winter walk.

1 If using dried beans, soak them in cold water for 5–6 hours or overnight, then drain, cover with fresh cold water and simmer for 35–40 minutes until they are cooked through.

2 Sauté the bacon in 2 tablespoons of olive oil in a flameproof casserole on a medium–high heat for a few minutes until golden. Add the garlic and cook for a few seconds, then add the tomatoes and the stock and simmer for 10 minutes.

3 Add the cooked, drained beans, then add the cabbage and sliced sausage and cook for a further 4 minutes. Add the chopped herbs, taste and correct the seasoning.

Childhood Favourites

We all have those special foods that conjure up warm, nostalgic feelings of childhood – meals that instantly transport you back in time in just one bite, whether they're the favourite dinners you begged your mum to make (and still do), or the treats that you used to create with cherished family members. For me, every time I eat poached egg on buttery toast I think of nothing but my dad's great weekend breakfasts before I went off to a hockey match. It's amazing quite how powerful and wonderful these taste memories can be. These are a few favourites from my own family – perhaps they'll become yours too.

Dad's Brown Bread

**MAKES 2 X 900G
(2LB) LOAVES**
VEGETARIAN

Sunflower oil, for greasing
350g (12oz) wholemeal flour
350g (12oz) plain flour
75g (3oz) bran
50g (2oz) wheatgerm
50g (2oz) pinhead oatmeal
    or oats
50g (2oz) brown sugar
1½ tsp salt
2 tsp baking powder
1 tsp bicarbonate of soda
2 eggs
1 litre (1¾ pints) buttermilk

My dad cooked few things when we were growing up, but he was famous for his amazing brown bread. I love big, thick slices of it, buttered and spread with jam. Though you can halve the quantities to make just one loaf, I usually make two loaves and freeze one.

1 Preheat the oven to 200°C (400°F), Gas mark 6.
2 Grease 2 x 900g (2lb) loaf tins with sunflower oil or line with parchment or non-stick paper.
3 Place the flours, bran, wheatgerm, oatmeal, sugar and salt in a large bowl. Sift in the baking powder and bicarbonate of soda. Mix thoroughly.
4 Whisk the eggs in a separate bowl and add the buttermilk. Make a well in the centre of the dry ingredients and pour in the eggs and buttermilk. Using one hand with your fingers open and stiff, mix in a full circle, bringing the flour and liquid together. The dough should be soft and sloppy.
5 Divide the dough between the prepared tins and place in the centre of the oven. Bake for 1 hour, then remove the bread from the tin and place back in the oven again without the tins for another 10–15 minutes until the loaves sound hollow when you tap them on the bottom.

Rachel's handy tip

If you slice your bread before you freeze it, then all you have to do is take a piece out of the freezer whenever you want toast.

Baked Cheesy Pasta

My sister and I absolutely loved this kind of cheesy pasta when growing up, and now I make it for my children. Sometimes I add chopped parsley. This can be prepared in advance and baked just before you are ready to eat.

1 Preheat the oven to 180°C (350°F), Gas mark 4.
2 Cook the pasta according to the instructions on the packet. Drain.
3 Meanwhile, place the cream and stock in another saucepan and bring to the boil. Take off the heat and add the mustard, the Gruyère and Cheddar cheeses and half of the Parmesan. Stir to melt all the cheese. Season with some pepper (it may not need any salt). Pour into the drained pasta and stir to mix.
4 Pour into a 25cm (10in) square or similar rectangular ovenproof gratin dish and sprinkle with the remaining Parmesan cheese. When you are ready to eat, place the dish in the oven and cook for 15–20 minutes or until brown on top and bubbling around the sides.

SERVES 4–6
VEGETARIAN
375g (13oz) dried pasta, such as conchiglie shells, fusilli or macaroni
300ml (½ pint) single cream
125ml (4fl oz) vegetable or chicken stock
1 tsp Dijon mustard
150g (5oz) Gruyère cheese, grated
150g (5oz) Cheddar cheese, grated
50g (2oz) Parmesan cheese, grated
Freshly ground black pepper

Old-fashioned Lemonade

This lemonade always reminds me of long, hot summers spent outdoors without a care in the world. The honey adds a much more interesting flavour than sugar. You can add fresh lime juice if you wish, but I love the simple lemon and honey flavours.

1 Place the honey and 60ml (2fl oz) of the water in a saucepan and heat up just enough to liquefy the honey. Then pour into a jug and allow to cool slightly.
2 Add the rest of the water together with the lemon juice and serve with ice.

MAKES 750ML (1¼ PINTS)
VEGETARIAN
150g (5oz) honey
600ml (1 pint) water
Juice of 4 lemons

TO SERVE
Ice

Sesame Goujons of Fish with Mushy Peas and Oven Roast Chips

Fish 'n' chips are a rite of passage. They're such a great and simple combination, and so universally loved. How can you eat mushy peas and not feel like a six-year-old again? The finger-size goujons and the sesame seeds just add a little twist to this old favourite.

SERVES 4

4–6 fillets (about 450g/1lb) of plaice or lemon sole
Sunflower oil, for frying
300ml (½ pint) milk
100g (4oz) plain flour
Pinch of salt
3 tbsp sesame seeds

FOR THE OVEN ROAST CHIPS

4–8 potatoes, peeled
30ml (1fl oz) olive oil

FOR THE MUSHY PEAS

225g (8oz) peas (can be frozen)
15g (½oz) butter or 1 tbsp olive oil

1 Prepare the fish by cutting it lengthways or at an angle into goujons (finger-sized pieces), about 1cm (½in) wide and 10cm (4in) long. Place the fish in a small bowl with the milk. Place the flour, salt and sesame seeds in another bowl. Preheat the oven to 220°C (425°F), Gas mark 7.

2 To make the oven roast chips, cut the peeled potatoes into chips, about 1cm (½in) wide. Place in a medium-sized saucepan, cover with boiling water from the kettle and boil for 1 minute, drain and spread out on kitchen paper to dry. Put the dried potatoes in a bowl and toss with the olive oil, spread out in a single layer in a baking tray and cook in the oven for 15–20 minutes or until golden and cooked.

3 Meanwhile, make the mushy peas. Bring a medium-sized saucepan with 500ml (18fl oz) water to the boil, drop in the peas, cover with the lid just until the water comes back to the boil on a high heat. Then remove the lid and boil for 1–2 minutes until the peas are just cooked but still bright green. Immediately drain them (reserving some of the liquid) and whiz them in a food processor with the butter or olive oil; you may need to add a tiny drop of the cooking liquid or cream if the mixture is too thick. Return the mushy peas to a saucepan for reheating later.

4 Next cook the fish. Heat a deep fat fryer with sunflower oil or a large sauté pan with about 2cm (¾in) oil. Take the fish out of the milk and drop it into the sesame flour. Toss it in the flour to completely cover each piece of fish and carefully place the fish into the pan of hot oil. Turn them after a minute and cook for 1 minute more – when the flour coating is golden, the fish should be cooked.

5 To serve, place the crispy goujons of fish on plates with the oven roast chips and mushy peas.

Irish Stew

The definitive recipe for Irish stew simply doesn't exist as in the past each household would have had its own family recipe. It is said, however, that people in the south of Ireland always add carrots, but people north of County Tipperary do not. Many people make their stew by placing alternate layers of meat, onions, carrots and potatoes in a pot, seasoned with salt and pepper, covered with water and stewed gently for a couple of hours. If you sear the meat and vegetables before stewing, as we do at Ballymaloe, it seals in the delicious sweet flavour.

1 Preheat the oven to 160°C (325°F), Gas mark 3.

2 Cut the chops in half, but keep the bones intact as they will give great flavour. Heat a medium–large ovenproof casserole pot or large saucepan with the olive oil until hot, then toss in the meat and cook for a minute on either side until it is nice and brown. Remove the meat and set aside and then cook the carrots and onions in the hot oil for a couple of minutes, seasoning with salt and pepper. Return the meat to the pot.

3 Add the stock and bring to the boil. Put the potatoes and sprig of thyme on top and transfer to the oven for 1½–2 hours or until the meat is very tender. When it is cooked, pour off the cooking liquid and allow it to sit for a minute until the fat floats to the top – adding a cube of ice will help speed this up. Spoon off the fat and pour the juices back over the stew. Add the chopped herbs and serve.

Rachel's handy tip

If the potatoes are quite small, add them 20–30 minutes after the stew starts cooking to avoid them breaking up.

SERVES 4–6

1.5kg (3lb 5oz) mutton chops from the neck or shoulder, still on the bone, cut about 1.5cm (¾in) thick

3 tbsp olive oil

3 carrots, peeled and cut into thick slices at an angle, or 12 small baby carrots, scrubbed and left whole

12 baby onions, peeled, or 3–4 medium onions, cut into quarters through the root, which should keep the wedges intact

Salt and freshly ground black pepper

400ml (14fl oz) lamb or chicken stock or water

8–12 potatoes, peeled and halved if very large

Sprig of thyme

1 tbsp chopped fresh parsley

1 tbsp snipped fresh chives

Pork Chops with Apple Sauce and Mustard Mash

SERVES 4–6

FOR THE MUSTARD MASH
Follow the Perfect Mash recipe
    on page 27
2–3 tbsp grainy mustard
Salt and freshly ground black
    pepper

FOR THE APPLE SAUCE
1 large cooking apple
    (350g/12oz), peeled, cored
    and roughly chopped
1 tbsp water
Tiny pinch cinnamon
    (optional)
25–50g (1–2oz) caster sugar

FOR THE PORK CHOPS
1–2 pork chops per person
Olive oil

This is just such a wonderful, old-fashioned family favourite and is destined to be so forever. I remember it well from our own family dinners. My mum used to serve the mustard and the mash separately on the plate and I would mix the mustard into the mash, even though this wasn't her intent! It's now evolved and I serve it as 'mustard mash', demonstrating that family recipes often change over time.

1 First prepare the mash on page 27, then stir in the grainy mustard to taste and add some salt and pepper.

2 Next make the apple sauce. Place the apple in a small saucepan with the water. Put the lid on and cook over a gentle heat (stir every now and then) until the apple has broken down to a mush. Add the cinnamon, if using, and sugar to taste. Serve warm or at room temperature.

3 To cook the chops, remove excess fat from the chops and then drizzle with olive oil and freshly ground black pepper. Place a large frying pan on a high heat. When it's good and hot, add the pork chops and sprinkle with a little sea salt. Cook for approximately 5 minutes on each side. Remove to a plate, cover and rest in a warm oven for 5 minutes.

4 To assemble, remove excess fat from the chops if you wish and place the chops on a serving plate with some mustard mash and a little apple sauce on the side.

Flapjacks

MAKES 25–30 FLAPJACKS
VEGETARIAN
350g (12oz) butter
2 generous tbsp golden syrup
175g (6oz) light muscovado
   or soft light brown sugar
1 tsp vanilla extract
75g (3oz) plain flour
375g (13oz) oats

These flapjacks really remind me of when I was little, cooking with my sister and mum. The flapjacks were never safe from us – we used to eat most of them before they had even cooled! Perfect with a glass of cold milk.

1 Preheat the oven to 180°C (350°F), Gas mark 4.

2 Place the butter, golden syrup, sugar and vanilla extract in a large saucepan. Bring up to a simmer and stir, allowing the butter to melt. When the mixture is smooth, take off the heat and add in the flour and the oats. Stir to mix and spread into a Swiss roll tin measuring 25 x 38cm (10 x 15in).

3 Bake in the oven (not too close to the top or it will burn) for 20–25 minutes or until golden. Cut into squares or fingers while still warm. Remove from the tin carefully while they are still slightly warm and allow to cool on a wire rack.

Variations

This is a great basic recipe to which you can add the following for a change:

Fruity flapjacks: 100g (4oz) of raisins, sultanas or chopped dates – or even chocolate chips!

Banana flapjacks: 1 mashed banana added into the wet ingredients (also good with chocolate chips!).

Flapjacks with seeds: 75g (3oz) seeds, such as pumpkin or sesame.

Ginger flapjacks: 75g (3oz) finely chopped crystallised ginger.

Banana and Chocolate Bread and Butter Pudding

This is a variation of classic basic bread and butter pudding that my mum used to make for me as a special treat, particularly if I was feeling under the weather. The banana flavour isn't overpowering, it just adds a delicious sweetness.

1 Spread a very thin layer of chocolate spread on the slices of bread. Arrange four slices, chocolate-side down in a 25cm (10in) square or similar rectangular gratin dish, or a similar-sized dish. Top with another four slices of bread, chocolate-side down, and finish with the last four slices, also chocolate-side down.

2 Place the cream and milk in a saucepan and bring to just under the boil.

3 While they are heating up, whisk the eggs, salt and sugar in a medium-sized bowl. Mash the bananas on a plate with a fork and add them to the eggs, then whisk in the hot cream and milk. Pour this custard over the bread and leave to soak for 10 minutes. When you are ready to cook, sprinkle the sugar over the top.

4 Meanwhile, preheat the oven to 180°C (350°F), Gas mark 4.

5 Place the gratin dish in a bain-marie (a larger ovenproof dish that has enough water in it to go 2.5cm [1in] up the sides of the gratin dish) and cook in the oven for 45–50 minutes or until it feels just set in the centre. Remove from the oven and serve warm with a light dusting of cocoa powder and some softly whipped cream, if you wish.

Rachel's handy tip

If you want to prepare this pudding a day ahead of serving, don't heat up the cream and milk – just pour it cold over the bread and store in the fridge until ready to cook.

SERVES 4–6
VEGETARIAN
2 tbsp chocolate spread
12 slices of white bread, crusts removed
350ml (12fl oz) single cream
350ml (12fl oz) milk
4 eggs
Pinch of salt
100g (4oz) caster sugar
2 bananas
2 tbsp granulated sugar, for topping

TO SERVE
Cocoa powder
Softly whipped cream (optional)

Ballymaloe Balloons

MAKES ABOUT 12 BALLOONS
VEGETARIAN
140g (scant 5oz) plain flour
2–4 tsp caster sugar, plus
    25g (1oz) for tossing
    the balloons
Pinch of salt
1 level tsp baking powder
200ml (7fl oz) milk

'Balloons' are like doughnuts and are one of my husband, Isaac's, very favourite childhood treats. This is a recipe from Isaac's grandmother, Myrtle Allen, who used to make these with her own mother when she was a child. She made them regularly for all the Allen grandchildren, and she still quite often makes these for the little guests staying at Ballymaloe for children's tea (and occasionally still for Isaac!). They're very simple and quick to make.

1 Heat a deep fat fryer to 190°C (375°F). Place the dry ingredients in a bowl and whisk to mix. Add the milk gradually, whisking all the time until you have a thick batter.

2 When the oil is hot in the deep fat fryer, take a dessertspoonful of the mixture and push it off gently using another spoon, so that it drops in a round ball into the oil. Repeat with the remaining batter to make about 12 balloons. Fry until deep golden, about 4–5 minutes, turning over halfway through cooking. Remove, drain on kitchen paper and toss in caster sugar (I sometimes add some ground cinnamon to the sugar), and serve warm.

Rachel's handy tip

If you don't have a deep fat fryer, you can fry the balloons in a wide sauté pan in the same way as the Sesame Goujons of Fish on page 42.

Rhubarb and Custard Tart

SERVES 4–6
VEGETARIAN

FOR THE PASTRY
150g (5oz) plain flour
25g (1oz) icing sugar
100g (4oz) butter
1 egg, whisked

FOR THE FILLING
4 egg yolks
4 generous tbsp honey
   (about 100g/4oz)
300ml (1/2 pint) double cream
225g (8oz) rhubarb, trimmed
   and sliced into 2cm (3/4in)
   lengths (if the stalks are
   very wide, cut them in
   half lengthways first)

Rhubarb and custard make such a great old-fashioned combination, and I love making them into a tart. As a child, we always made this with our own rhubarb, fresh from the garden. We always knew summer was approaching when the first rhubarb appeared.

1 First, make the pastry. Place the flour and icing sugar in a medium-sized bowl. Rub in the butter, then add most of the egg (you probably won't need it all) to make the dough come together. Add a tablespoon of water to the remaining egg to make egg wash, and reserve. Slightly flatten the pastry, cover and place in the fridge for about 30 minutes (or 10 minutes in the freezer), until chilled.

2 Preheat the oven to 180°C (350°F), Gas mark 4. Grease a 23cm (9in) shallow tart tin with a removable base with a little butter.

3 When you are ready to roll out the pastry, remove it from the fridge and place between two sheets of cling film that are larger than your tart tin. Using a rolling pin, roll out the pastry until it's about 5mm (1/4in) thick and large enough to line the base and sides of the prepared tin. Remove the top layer of cling film and place the pastry upside down (cling film side facing up) in the tart tin. Press into the edges, cling film still attached, and, using your thumb, 'cut' the pastry on the edge of the tin to give a neat finish. Remove the cling film and pop the pastry in the freezer for at least 10 minutes.

4 Next, 'blind bake' the pastry case to partially cook it before adding its filling. Line the pastry with greaseproof paper (leaving plenty to come up the sides), fill with baking beans or dried pulses (you can use these over and over), and bake for about 10 minutes in the oven, until the pastry feels dry. Remove the paper and beans, brush with a little egg white and return to the oven for 4–5 minutes. Take out of the oven and put to one side while you prepare the filling.

5 In a medium-sized bowl, whisk the yolks with the honey, add the cream and mix. Pour the custard into the case almost to the top, then arrange the rhubarb on top. It can be easier to do all this while the case is sitting on a rack in the oven to avoid spilling the mixture. Bake for 30 minutes or until just set. Let cool to room temperature.

Making Memories

So many of our own memories of childhood often centre around the kitchen. One of the joys of being an adult is sharing those experiences with our own children and teaching them new skills that they will hopefully pass on to their own children. Even simple tasks, such as mashing potatoes, can plant the seeds for future memories. It's more about spending time together and helping children gain confidence which will carry over into so many other parts of their lives. It helps to choose recipes in which they can take an active part or get creative so they can be proud of their work. Have fun and enjoy!

Cheesy Sodabread

All children love playing with dough, and with this Irish soda bread dough you can be as creative as you like. I often leave out the herbs; sometimes I leave out the cheese and replace the herbs with a handful of chopped milk or dark chocolate, or even raisins or dried cranberries. These scones can be cut into any shapes that your little ones like, though if handled and kneaded too much they will get slightly tough.

1 Preheat the oven to 250°C (475°F), Gas mark 9.
2 Sieve the dry ingredients into a bowl, then mix in the chopped herbs. Make a well in the centre. Pour in all the milk at once. Using one hand, with your fingers outstretched like a claw, stir in a full circular movement from the centre to the outside of the bowl. The dough should be softish, though not too wet and sticky.
3 When the dough comes together, turn it out onto a well-floured surface. Pat the dough until it is about 2cm (3/4in) thick. Cut into round or square shapes about the size of a scone, then place on a floured baking tray. Generously sprinkle each sodabread scone with the grated cheese.
4 Place the tray in the oven. Cook for 10–20 minutes (depending on size) until golden and sounding hollow when tapped on the bottom. Turn the oven down to 200°C (400°F), Gas mark 6 after 10 minutes if they are already golden.

Variations
To make chocolate chip sodabread, omit the cheese and replace the herbs with 75–100g (3–4oz) of chopped dark or milk chocolate or chocolate chips. You could also add an egg to the buttermilk and 1 tablespoon of caster sugar to increase the richness. It's also delicious with 100g (4oz) of raisins or dried cranberries.

MAKES ABOUT 16 SCONES
VEGETARIAN
450g (1lb) plain white flour
1 level tsp salt
1 level tsp bicarbonate of soda
1 tbsp chopped fresh herbs, such as rosemary, thyme, sage, parsley or chives
400ml (14fl oz) buttermilk or sour milk (to sour milk, add 3 generous tbsp natural yoghurt or juice from 1/2 lemon to 400ml/14fl oz fresh milk)
About 75g (3oz) Cheddar or Gruyère cheese, grated

Wholemeal Honey Bread

MAKES 2 x 900G (2LB) LOAVES

VEGETARIAN

450ml (16fl oz) warm water
3 tbsp honey
3 tsp dried or fast-acting yeast
    or 40g (1¾oz) fresh yeast
600g (1lb 7oz) strong white
    flour
300g (11oz) wholemeal flour
2 tsp salt
100g (4oz) butter, cut
    into cubes

Making yeast bread from scratch is becoming a lost art, but it is the perfect thing both for teaching new skills and for having fun with your children. Even if you've never made bread before, why not spend the time together as a family learning to get it right? Children always have such fun watching and waiting for the dough to rise and then punching it down. Although you should put aside a whole morning or afternoon for this, you'll be able to get on with plenty of other things while the bread is rising. This is a simple and tasty bread, and once you have mastered it you'll want to move on to other flavours and combinations (see variations, opposite).

1 In a small bowl, mix the warm water with the honey, add the yeast and leave to stand for 5 minutes until slightly frothy.
2 Place the flours in a big mixing bowl (or the bowl of an electric food mixer) and mix in the salt and then rub in the butter. Pour most of the frothy liquid into the flour and mix to a dough – it should not be too wet and sticky; if it's too dry, add more warm water and if it's too wet, add more flour.
3 Knead by hand on a floured surface or in the mixer for about 10 minutes (it may only take 5 minutes in the mixer) until the dough is smooth and springy. Place in a lage oiled bowl, cover with cling film and leave somewhere warm (like a warm spot in your kitchen) for 2–3 hours until it's doubled in size. It has risen enough when it does not spring back when you push your finger onto the dough.
4 When it's risen, knock it back by punching it down in the bowl (my children love this bit!) and kneading on the floured surface for 1 minute. Allow to rest on the work surface, covered with a tea towel for 5 minutes before shaping it. I usually shape this into two round or oval loaves but, of course, you can make individual rolls if you wish (you would get about 20 rolls). Slash the loaves four or five times over the top with a sharp knife (I don't do this with rolls). Do make sure you flatten the loaves and rolls to about 4cm (1½in) high because they will rise.
5 Preheat the oven to 200°C (400°F), Gas mark 6.

6 Place the loaves on a floured baking tray, sprinkle with flour and cover with a tea towel and allow to rise (this may take another 45 minutes) and, again, leave somewhere warm until they have doubled in size. The dough has risen enough when it does not spring back when you push your finger onto it.

7 Remove the tea towel and bake the bread in the oven for 30–40 minutes or until it sounds hollow when tapped on the base. The rolls will only take about 10–15 minutes to cook. Leave to cool on a wire rack.

Variations

If you don't want to use brown flour, you can use 900g (2lb) white strong flour in its place. You can also add other flavours and ingredients after you've knocked back the dough while you are giving it its final kneading. The main ingredients remain the same so the quantities are up to you, the fun is in the experimentation. Try to come up with your own family recipe or try these great flavours and combinations:

- Cheese – choose a good melting variety like Gruyère or Cheddar, or a combination, and sprinkle a bit on top as well
- Caramelised onions and blue cheese
- Walnuts and raisins (or other dried fruit)
- Cinnamon and raisins
- Caraway seeds
- Spices, such as turmeric
- Chopped olives
- Sun-dried tomatoes
- Pesto, but try not to mix it in too much
- Pine nuts
- Chopped herbs

Fruity Pancakes

MAKES ABOUT 12 PANCAKES
VEGETARIAN
150g (5oz) plain flour
2 tsp baking powder
¼ tsp bicarbonate of soda
25–50g (1–2oz) caster sugar
2 eggs
100–125ml (3½–4fl oz)
    buttermilk
25g (1oz) butter, melted
The fruit of your choice, about
    125–150g (4½–5oz) in total,
    or 1 large, 1½ medium or 2
    small bananas, mashed
    (150g/5oz mashed weight)
Sunflower oil

SERVING SUGGESTIONS
Chocolate spread
Maple syrup or golden syrup
Fruit, such as raspberries,
    blueberries or chopped
    strawberries
Lemon juice and icing sugar

Putting fruit into pancakes is a great way of getting fruit into your kids! Let them choose their favourites (although soft fruits work best), and they can even make their own patterns with brightly coloured fruit such as blueberries and raspberries. My children love helping to make pancakes, and particularly like them with mashed banana with chocolate spread on top (for special occasions). These pancakes are thick and fluffy, like American pancakes, and are great for breakfast, brunch or a mid-afternoon treat.

1 Sift the flour, baking powder and bicarbonate of soda together in a bowl. Add the caster sugar and mix.

2 In another bowl whisk the eggs, then add the buttermilk and melted butter. Pour this into the dry ingredients, whisking as you add it in. The batter is ready to use now or may be stored in the fridge overnight.

3 If you are using mashed banana, fold it in just before you want to cook the pancakes.

4 Heat a large frying pan over a medium heat and oil it very lightly (I usually just rub it with an oiled piece of kitchen paper). Drop large spoonfuls (about 60ml/2fl oz) of pancake batter into the hot pan. Leave plenty of space between them as they spread while cooking. If you want to add other fruit, such as the berries, do so now. Don't mix it in, just place it on top of the cooking batter.

5 Cook for 1–2 minutes on the first side until bubbles appear on the upper surface, then use a fish slice or something similar to turn the pancakes over and finish cooking on the second side for another couple of minutes until golden brown. Cook all the pancakes this way. Serve with sliced strawberries and dredge with icing sugar.

Homemade Pizzas with Quick Yeast Dough

MAKES ABOUT 12 25CM
(10IN) DIAMETER PIZZAS

FOR THE PIZZA DOUGH
700g (1½lb) strong white flour
1 rounded tsp salt
1 tbsp sugar
50g (2oz) butter
15g packet (2 x 7½g sachets)
    fast-acting yeast
3 tbsp olive oil, plus extra
    for brushing
350–400ml (12–14fl oz)
    lukewarm water

FOR THE TOMATO SAUCE
600g (1lb 7oz) ripe fresh
    tomatoes, halved
3 cloves of garlic, peeled
    and kept whole
5 tbsp olive oil
3 tbsp balsamic vinegar
Salt, freshly ground black
    pepper and sugar

YOUR FAVOURITE TOPPINGS,
SUCH AS:
Mozzarella (approximately
    450g (1lb) for 12 pizzas)
Slices of chorizo or pepperoni
    sausage
Small florets of broccoli
Cherry tomatoes
Peppers
Small red onions
Olives and anchovies (if your
    children like them)

Our children love making pizzas, and it keeps them amused for ages because they can choose their own toppings and create their own designs. This recipe has less salt and sugar than most shop-bought pizzas, and no hidden additives. Place as many toppings as you need in individual bowls and let the children make up their own combinations – with a little guidance, if necessary.

1 First, make the pizza dough. Place the flour, salt and sugar in a big mixing bowl. Rub in the butter, add the yeast and mix together. Make a well in the centre of the dry ingredients, add the oil and most, but not all, of the warm water and mix to a loose dough. Add more water or flour, if needed.

2 Take the dough out of the bowl and let it sit on a lightly floured worktop, covered with a tea towel, for 5 minutes. Then knead the dough for 10 minutes or until it feels smooth and slightly springy. You can also do this in a food mixer with the dough hook – it takes half the time. Let the dough relax for a few minutes again.

3 Shape and measure into 12 equal balls of dough, each weighing about 100g (4oz). Lightly brush the balls of dough with olive oil. If you have time, cover the oiled dough with cling film and put into the fridge for 30 minutes. The dough will be easier to handle when cold but it can also be used immediately.

4 Preheat oven to 230°C (450°F), Gas mark 8.

5 To make the sauce, lay the tomatoes on a baking tray, cut side up. Add the garlic, drizzle with olive oil and balsamic vinegar, and season with salt, pepper and sugar. Cook in the oven for 20–30 minutes, until the tomatoes are completely soft and blistered. Remove and liquidise and strain. Season again to taste. The sauce needs to be thick enough to coat the back of a spoon. If it needs thickening, place in a saucepan, bring to the boil and reduce to thicken, which could take up to 10 minutes.

6 Prepare your toppings. Grate the mozzarella; boil the broccoli florets in water until just al dente (about 5 minutes), then drain

and plunge into iced water to refresh; halve the cherry tomatoes; deseed and slice the peppers into strips and quarter the red onions, then roast in the hot oven for 10 minutes with a drizzle of olive oil, thyme leaves, salt and pepper.

7 Place on a flat sheet or an upside-down baking tray in the oven – it's easier to slide the pizza on and off if the surface does not have a lip. Then, on a floured work surface, roll each ball of dough out to a disc about 25cm (10in) in diameter – if you have semolina or fine polenta you can use this to dust your worktop instead of flour.

8 Place a pizza base on a second, cool upside-down floured tray, spread with a little tomato sauce and sprinkle with your chosen toppings and cheese.

9 Slide the pizza off the cool tray onto the hot tray in the centre of the oven and cook for 5–10 minutes, depending on the heat of the oven and the thickness of the pizza, until the pizza is golden underneath and bubbling on top. I find it best to cook just one or two pizzas at a time.

Joshua's Croque Monsieur

SERVES 4
25g (1oz) butter, plus extra
  for spreading
25g (1oz) plain flour
250ml (9fl oz) milk
1 generous tsp Dijon mustard
125g (4¹/₂oz) mature Gruyère
  or Emmental cheese, grated
2 egg yolks
1 French stick, cut in half
  lengthways and then each
  long slice cut in half
8 slices ham

My eldest son, Joshua, is nearly old enough to make this on his own, so he often asks for it when he wants to do a little cooking with me. This is just one step beyond a traditional toasted ham-and-cheese sandwich, but is substantial enough to make children feel as though they've helped to make a proper meal.

1 In a sauté pan, melt the butter and then add the flour and cook for a minute. Whisk in the milk gradually and cook for a minute until thickened. Take off the heat and add the mustard and grated cheese. Mix to melt the cheese, then whisk in the egg yolks.

2 Preheat a hot grill. Toast the crust side of the French stick under the grill. Remove, turn over and add butter and then a slice of ham on each un-toasted side. Spread the cheese sauce over the ham and place under the grill for 3–4 minutes, or until golden and bubbly.

Burgers with Guacamole and Crispy Bacon and Cucumber Relish

I always make up this quantity and freeze the extra uncooked burgers, but if you want to halve this recipe, just use 1 small egg. The guacamole is a great accompaniment to burgers, and it's another good way of getting your kids to eat something green.

⟶ · ◎ · ⟶

1 First make the relish, an hour ahead if possible. These ingredients make about 1 x 400g jar. Mix the cucumber and onion in a large bowl, add the sugar, salt and vinegar and mix well to combine. Store in a jar or a bowl in the fridge.

2 To make the guacamole, mash the avocado flesh, add all the other ingredients and lime or lemon juice to taste. Put the guacamole into a bowl and place a sheet of cling film on the surface to prevent it going brown. Keep until needed.

3 Now for the burgers. Place the olive oil in a saucepan, add the onion, season with salt and pepper, cover and sweat over a low heat for 10 minutes until completely cooked. Allow to cool. Then mix with the remaining ingredients and season to taste by tossing a tiny bit of the mixture in a hot pan so that it cooks before you try it for flavour. Shape into burgers and freeze or cook by placing on a pan on a medium heat and cooking on both sides for 6–8 minutes until cooked through.

4 Serve on toasted burger buns with guacamole and crispy bacon on top. Sometimes our children put little cubes of cheese (1cm/1/2in dice) into the centre of the burgers when they are shaping them, which melt all the way through as the burgers cook.

Rachel's handy tip ◎

If you prefer, you can start cooking the burgers in a pan for 1 or 2 minutes on each side until deep golden then pop in a hot oven on a baking tray for another 10 minutes until cooked through. Else, pop them on the barbeque for a great summer family dinner.

MAKES 8 BURGERS

FOR THE CUCUMBER RELISH
300g (11oz) unpeeled cucumber, thinly sliced
1 small onion, peeled and thinly sliced (optional)
100g (4oz) sugar
1 tsp salt
75ml (21/2fl oz) cider vinegar or white wine vinegar

FOR THE AVOCADO GUACAMOLE
2 ripe avocadoes, peeled and stone removed
2 cloves of garlic, peeled and crushed
2 tbsp olive oil (optional)
2 tbsp chopped fresh coriander or parsley
Sea salt and freshly ground black pepper
Juice of 1/2 lime or lemon

FOR THE BURGERS
2 tbsp olive oil
2 small onions, peeled and chopped
Salt and freshly ground black pepper
800g (1lb 12oz) minced beef
4 tbsp chopped fresh herbs, such as a mixture of tarragon, chives, thyme and parsley
4 cloves of garlic, peeled and crushed or grated
1 large egg, beaten
50g (2oz) breadcrumbs

TO SERVE
Toasted burger buns
2 rashers of crispy bacon per person

Lucca's Chicken Wings with Corn on the Cob and Shelled Peas

SERVES 4
12–16 chicken wings
4 tbsp sweet chilli sauce
4 tbsp soy sauce
2 generous tbsp brown sugar

FOR THE CORN ON THE COB
AND SHELLED PEAS
4 corn on the cob, cut in half
   if you wish
Sea salt
15g (1/2oz) butter, softened
250g (9oz) shelled peas (frozen
   are fine if you're pressed
   for time)

TO SERVE
1 tbsp toasted sesame seeds

This is one of the simplest things to cook, so much so that our family have named it after my youngest son, who helped create the recipe! If you have the time, one of the joys of this dinner is in getting everyone together to husk the corn and shell the peas. It also gives kids a chance to understand a bit more about where their food comes from and to see how it grows. So often when kids help prepare their food they're more likely to eat it!

1 Place the chicken wings in a bowl and add the sweet chilli sauce, soy sauce and sugar, and toss to mix. Leave the chicken to marinate for 2–3 hours, if possible (if you have just a half an hour, that will be fine). If you are using husked corn and unshelled peas, get these prepared for cooking first. You can even have a little healthy competition to see who can husk their corn the fastest or who can shell the most peas!

2 Preheat the oven to 220°C (425°F), Gas mark 7.

3 Spread out the wings and all the marinade in a single layer on an oven tray and cook in the oven for 18–22 minutes until golden brown and cooked through.

4 Meanwhile, cook the corn on the cob. Bring a saucepan of water up to the boil, add a pinch of salt and drop in the corn. Cook in boiling water on a medium heat for 6–10 minutes (depending on the size of the sweetcorn) until the kernels are cooked.

5 Likewise, cook the shelled peas. Bring a saucepan of water up to the boil, add a pinch of salt and drop in the peas. Cook in boiling water on a high heat for 2–3 minutes, until the peas are cooked. Drain immediately.

6 To serve, drain the corn on the cob, spread with a little butter and sprinkle with sea salt. Drain the peas. Transfer the vegetables to plates or bowls and add the chicken wings. Sprinkle the chicken with sesame seeds and allow to cool for a minute before eating.

Chocolate Chip Peanut Butter Cookies

All kids seem to adore these cookies (see the photograph on page 79) – they are so moreish (and adults love them too). This is a great quick recipe to make after school.

1 Preheat the oven to 180°C (350°F), Gas mark 4.

2 In a large bowl using a wooden spoon or in an electric mixer, beat the peanut butter, soft butter, sugar and vanilla extract until soft and creamy. Beat in the eggs, one at a time, then add the chocolate. Sift in the flour, bicarbonate of soda and salt and stir to mix.

3 Roll heaped teaspoonfuls of the dough in your hands to form balls, then place them spaced apart on baking trays (there is no need to grease or line them).

4 Bake in the oven for 12–16 minutes until light golden in colour. Carefully lift them off the trays when cooked and place on a wire rack to cool.

5 If you don't want to cook all the dough, place a sheet of greaseproof paper or cling film on the work surface and roll any spare dough into a log about 2cm (3/4in) in diameter. Roll up and place in the fridge. When you are ready to cook, unwrap the log and cut into slices about 8mm (3/8in) thick. Place on the baking trays and cook as above.

Rachel's handy tip

The recipe makes loads of cookies, but you don't have to cook them all at once. Just roll your dough into the log shapes and store in the fridge (for up to 1 week) or in the freezer for up to 3 months. You can then just cut slices off the frozen dough and pop them right on the tray when you're ready to cook. Of course, you can halve this recipe if you like.

MAKES ABOUT 60 COOKIES
VEGETARIAN

200g (7oz) crunchy peanut butter
200g (7oz) butter, softened
250g (9oz) light muscovado or soft light brown sugar
1 tsp vanilla extract
2 eggs
250g (9oz) chocolate, chopped
350g (12oz) plain flour
1 tsp bicarbonate of soda
Pinch of salt

Polka-dot Cookies

MAKES ABOUT 25 LARGE
COOKIES
VEGETARIAN

225g (8oz) butter
375g (15oz) soft light brown
   or light muscovado sugar
2 tsp vanilla extract
2 eggs, beaten
350g (14oz) plain flour
1/2 tsp salt
1 level tsp bicarbonate of soda
1 level tsp baking powder
150g (5oz) Smarties

These are seriously fun and pretty cookies. They are crisp on the outside and a bit chewy and gooey on the inside. Treat your children to them with a mug of hot chocolate or a glass of milk, and tell them stories about when you were little!

1 Preheat the oven to 180°C (350°F), Gas mark 4.

2 Cream the butter in a large bowl, add the sugar and beat until soft and light. Add the vanilla, then the eggs gradually while beating.

3 Place the flour and salt in a separate, medium-sized bowl and sift in the bicarbonate of soda and the baking powder, then mix. Add the dry ingredients to the wet ingredients and fold in, then add the Smarties and mix.

4 Form the dough into balls (to make big cookies, use a golf-ball size; for small ones, use small walnut size) and place them on baking trays (there's no need to grease or line them), allowing plenty of room for spreading.

5 Place the cookies in the oven. Small cookies take about 8 minutes and large ones about 13–16 minutes. They are cooked when they are golden around the edges and pale golden in the centre – they will still be a bit gooey and chewy if you cook them like this. For crisper cookies, bake until they are evenly golden all over. They often cook unevenly so keep checking them in the oven and take out the cooked ones.

6 Transfer carefully to a wire rack while hot, using a stainless-steel fish slice – if you let them cool on the baking trays they will stick.

Something to Celebrate

Congratulations! You've just become
engaged. You've just landed your dream
job. You've just had some incredible news
and want to splash out on the best that
money can buy to celebrate in serious style.
These are my top picks for luxury foods
or impressive dishes that you can make
at home. Admittedly, many of these
recipes contain expensive ingredients
and are therefore not for every day, but
nor should they be. These are foods that
say 'Hurray!' and are to be savoured
and appreciated for their sheer glamour
and delicious decadence.

Canapés

EACH RECIPE MAKES
ABOUT 20 CANAPÉS

MINIATURE STEAK SANDWICHES WITH GREEN MAYONNAISE AND SALSA

FOR THE HERB MAYONNAISE

Makes 150ml (1/4 pint)
1 egg yolk
Pinch of salt
1/2 tsp Dijon mustard
1 tsp white wine vinegar
90ml (3fl oz) sunflower oil
    and 30ml (1fl oz) olive oil
4 cloves of garlic, peeled and
    crushed or grated
1 tbsp each of chopped fresh
    rocket, watercress, parsley
    and tarragon

FOR THE TOMATO SALSA

2 tomatoes, chopped
1 clove of garlic, peeled
    and crushed or grated
A squeeze of lemon juice
1 tbsp finely chopped onion
Salt, freshly ground black
    pepper and a pinch of sugar

FOR THE STEAK

700g (1 1/2lb) sirloin (fat
    removed) or fillet steak, cut
    into slices 1cm (1/2in) thick
1–2 tbsp olive oil

TO SERVE

1 French stick, cut into
    1cm (1/2in) thick slices
    and toasted

Whether you're celebrating à deux or with a crowd, there's something special about treating your guests to something more interesting than a bowl of nuts before your meal! Canapés can really get the party (and the appetite) going, and are such a lovely unexpected extra. Here are two of my favourites, but the combinations are endless. Try experimenting with different ingredients to find your own favourites. You can also try making mini-versions of some of your favourite foods, like savoury pies and quiches. If you are hosting a drinks party and are not serving a sit-down dinner, you can follow your savoury canapés with elegant sweet ones, such as the White Chocolate Truffles with Cardamom on page 204.

Miniature Steak Sandwiches with Herb Mayonnaise and Salsa

1 First make the herb mayonnaise. Put the egg yolk into a mixing bowl, add the salt, mustard and vinegar and whisk together. Mix the oils together, then very gradually add the oils drop by drop to the egg yolks, whisking all the time. (I often use an electric hand blender.) When you have whisked in all the oil, it should look thick and creamy. Add salt to taste and then mix the mayonnaise with the garlic and chopped herbs.

2 Next make the salsa. In a bowl, mix together all the ingredients and season to taste.

3 Place the raw steaks on a work surface and using a round cutter slightly smaller than the slices of toast, stamp out circles of raw steak. Heat a frying pan until very hot, add olive oil and a single layer of steak rounds and then cook for approximately 1 minute on each side (depending on how you want it cooked). Remove from the pan and repeat with the remaining steaks until they are all cooked.

4 To serve, spread each piece of toast with the herb mayonnaise. Top each with a round of steak and half a teaspoon of salsa.

MINI MUSHROOM
BRUSCHETTA WITH ROCKET,
OLIVES AND PARMESAN
MAKES ABOUT 20 CANAPÉS
VEGETARIAN

1 French stick, preferably
    1 or 2 days old
125ml (4fl oz) olive oil
20 small flat mushrooms,
    wiped and stalks removed
4 cloves of garlic, peeled
    and crushed or grated
Salt and freshly ground
    black pepper
20 small rocket leaves
2 tbsp finely chopped
    pitted black olives
20 shavings of Parmesan
    cheese, using a peeler

Mini Mushroom Bruschetta with Rocket, Olives and Parmesan

1 Preheat the oven to 200°C (400°F), Gas mark 6.

2 Cut the French stick into 1cm (1/2in) slices. Place in a bowl, drizzle in half the olive oil and toss with your hands. Place the little slices in a single layer on a baking tray and cook in the oven for 4–5 minutes until slightly toasted. Remove from the oven and set aside. You can serve these warm or at room temperature.

3 Keep the oven on and place the flat mushrooms on a baking tray, also in a single layer. In a bowl, mix the garlic and the remaining olive oil and season with salt and pepper. Spoon this garlic oil over each mushroom (about a teaspoon for each) and roast in the oven for 8–10 minutes or until the mushrooms are cooked. These can be allowed to cool to room temperature.

4 To assemble, place the bruschettas on a large plate, top each with a rocket leaf, then a roasted mushroom, then a scattering of chopped olives. Top each with a Parmesan shaving and serve.

Spagettini with Caviar and Crème Fraîche

Caviar is considered the ultimate in extravagant foods, but fear not – there are lots of different grades, many of which are inexpensive, so you need not take out a second mortgage for this dish! Serving caviar with a delicate pasta in this way is one of the best ways of eating it. In many ways, the pasta enhances the flavour of the caviar because it doesn't compete, so a little goes a long way.

1 Cook the pasta as directed on the packet in a large pot of boiling water with the salt. While the pasta is cooking, place the fish stock in another saucepan and boil, uncovered, for 2–3 minutes until reduced by half.

2 Take off the heat, whisk in the crème fraîche, stir in the caviar and chopped herbs. Once the pasta is cooked, drain and mix with the caviar sauce and serve.

SERVES 4

400g (14oz) spagettini
   or spaghetti
1 tsp salt
200ml (7fl oz) fish stock
60ml (2fl oz) crème fraîche
2 tbsp caviar, plus a little extra
   for the top if you wish
1 tbsp chopped fresh parsley
1 tbsp snipped fresh chives

Hot Buttered Lobster

I could not write a chapter about food for special occasions without including the recipe for hot buttered lobster. This is the ultimate in decadent food.

1 A couple of hours before you are ready to cook, put the lobsters in a plastic bag and put in the freezer. When it is time to cook them, bring a large saucepan of salted water (3 tablespoons salt to every 2 litres of water) to the boil.

2 Plunge the frozen lobsters directly into the boiling water and when they start to turn from dark blue to browny orange (about 10 minutes), remove them from the pan and discard the water.

3 Put the carrot, onion, celery, water, wine, herbs and peppercorns into the same saucepan and bring to the boil. Add the lobsters and cover with the lid. Cook until they turn a very bright orange-red with no trace of blue: for 900g (2lb) of lobster, this will be about 20 minutes and for 1.3kg (3lb) of lobster, this will be about 30 minutes. When they are cooked, take them out of the pot and sit somewhere to cool. Strain the cooking liquid and use as fish stock (it will freeze).

4 Once the lobsters are cool enough to handle, take a large, sharp chopping knife and cut them in half along the top from the head to the tail as evenly as possible. Extract all the brown meat from the head and the white meat from the tail and claws. You will need to use either a wooden mallet or the flat edge of a chopping knife blade to crack open the claws. Chop the meat into 2cm (3/4in) chunks.

5 Clean the lobster shells (keep the head and tail intact, if possible, to serve the lobster in) and pop into an oven to heat up.

6 Melt the butter in a frying pan on a high heat. When it's hot and foaming, add the lobster meat and toss for about a minute. Season with lemon juice and pepper. Using a slotted spoon, divide the lobster between the half shells on warmed plates, then spoon the juices over the lobster meat. Serve immediately with wedges of lemon and see your guests melt in ecstasy!

SERVES 4

2 x 900g (2lb) live lobsters
Salt and freshly ground
    black pepper
1 carrot, peeled and sliced
1 onion, peeled and sliced
2 celery stalks, sliced
600ml (1 pint) water
600ml (1 pint) dry white wine
A couple of sprigs of fresh
    parsley and thyme
1 bay leaf
A few peppercorns
50g (2oz) butter
Juice of 1 lemon, plus wedges
    to garnish

Langoustines with Brétonne Sauce

SERVES 4
2 egg yolks
1 tsp Dijon mustard
2 tsp white wine vinegar
2 generous tsp finely chopped
   fresh herbs, such as a
   mixture of parsley, tarragon,
   fennel and chives
100g (4oz) butter
20–28 fresh langoustines,
   preferably raw

TO SERVE
Toast (optional)

This has to be one of my favourite ways to eat langoustines (also known as Dublin Bay prawns). They look so beautiful on the plate, and when served whole they make a real statement, fitting for a special meal. The rich and divine Brétonne sauce is very easy to make and is similar to hollandaise. Choose really lovely, fresh langoustines (not frozen tiger prawns).

1 To make the sauce, place the egg yolks in a bowl and add the mustard, wine vinegar and the chopped herbs. Melt 75g (3oz) of the butter in a small saucepan and allow to boil. Place the egg yolks in a medium-sized bowl and gradually pour the melted butter onto the egg yolks, whisking all the time so that the sauce emulsifies and thickens. Keep warm by placing the sauce in a bowl or jug and sit in hot (but not boiling) water. The sauce will keep perfectly like this for a couple of hours – keep heating up the water if it cools down.

2 Boil the langoustines in salted water over a high heat until they float and turn an opaque pink, which will take about 2 minutes. When they seem done, break the head off of one to test that the flesh is also opaque. If the flesh isn't opaque, cook the langoustines for a further 30 seconds and test again.

3 Arrange the langoustines on warm plates and serve with the Brétonne sauce in little bowls on the plates or on the side and slices of warm toast, if using.

Choosing wine

Choosing wine can be quite fun, but many people feel a bit intimidated, particularly when dining with others who may be more knowledgeable. Remember that you do not have to be an expert to ask questions and it is never too late to learn!

In the same way that food follows trends, so too does wine. One year a certain wine will be all the rage, the next it may be passé. I feel it's pointless to rule out a whole category of wine completely because of fashion, so don't be afraid to stick with what you love.

The cost of wine is of course a major factor when making your choices, but high price does not necessarily equate to better flavour. There are many reasons why a particular wine may be expensive and rarity often comes in to the equation. However, sometimes the best does really come at a cost. Still, there are many, many delicious and desirable wines for under £10/€13. A good wine merchant will be more than happy to help steer you in the right direction and may even let you sample certain wines. Just leave your car at home!

One other thing worth noting is that until fairly recently screw caps were the hallmark of cheap and nasty wine. Today it's not surprising to see screw caps on some very fine wines indeed. They're often considered more reliable than corks in preventing oxygen from altering the flavour, and also in preventing mould. More and more producers are opting for screw caps, so although they're not as romantic, they are certainly nothing to be ashamed of.

The obvious place to start in choosing wine is to match the tone of your wine to that of your meal. Thus, pair hearty food with hearty wine and light food with light wine. A very general but useful tip that works more often than not is to match the food of a country or region with wine from that the same place. It therefore goes without saying that most Italian wines will match well with food such as pizza, pasta or risotto. Simple but true!

Red wines Red wine is produced by fermenting the juice of red or black grapes along with their flesh and skins. The skin contains the colour and tannins.

Red wines range from light and fruity such as Valpolicella, Beaujolais or even Rioja, to mid-weight wines such as Burgundy and Pinot Noir, through to rich reds that are high in tannin such as Bordeaux, Barolo, Barbera, Barbaresco, Merlot or Cabernet Sauvignon.

The lighter reds go very well with pasta and vegetable-based dishes. The mid-weight reds complement meats such as roast lamb. The truly hearty reds are perfect with red meat such as beef or venison. However, red wine is not just for red meat and works surprisingly well with fish, such as Cabernet Sauvignon with pan-fried salmon, Barolo with sea bass, or Pinot Noir with grilled mussels and garlic breadcrumbs.

White wines In the production of white wine the juice is fermented after the skins and flesh of the grapes have been filtered out, so that white can actually be produced from any colour of grape. However, a white wine made from a very dark grape may appear slightly pink, or 'blush'.

Whites, as we know, can range from bone dry to very sweet, with spicy, buttery and fruity flavours along the way. If you want a glass of fresh, crisp and not-too-demanding wine at lunchtime, try Soave or Pinot Grigio. With salads, chicken or seafood try fruity Sauvignon Blanc or a dry, well-balanced Muscadet. The aromatic Gewurtztraminer can stand up to spicy food and roast pork, as can many slightly sweet Reislings. Almondy, buttery, unoaked Chardonnays (like Chablis), Voigniers and dry Riesling are all fantastic with rich seafood such as lobster or scallops.

Rosé wines Rosé begins its life in the same way as red, but after a short time the skins are filtered out rather than left in throughout fermentation. This leaves it tasting more akin to white wine, but retaining some tint. The colour can vary quite a lot depending on the grape and the processing, but will always be characteristically pink.

After its huge popularity in the Seventies, rosé developed a reputation for being naff. However, in France and Spain it has always remained a popular lunch-time drink. Perhaps due to the rise in continental second homes, rosé is having a renaissance. It is now seen for the fun, light wine that it is; great for glugging joyfully on a summer's day.

The qualities I look for in a good rosé are crispness and freshness. Buy the youngest that you can find with a good balance of fruitiness and acidity. As well as the Spanish and French rosés, check out those from Chile or Australia.

Champagne/sparkling wines Though there is often nothing like a glass of chilled champagne, do not dismiss the other bubblies. The word 'champagne' does not necessarily mean it will be good quality; cheap champagne can be less desirable than many carefully made non-champagne sparklers.

Champagne and sparkling wines contain carbon dioxide, which is either naturally produced during fermentation or added later. To qualify as true champagne it must be produced only in the Champagne region of north-eastern France. Sparkling wines, on the other hand, are made in many countries and are often known by their regional names, such as Cava from Spain, Spumante or Prosecco from Italy and Sekt or Schaumwein from Germany. Sparkling wines are also made in California, Australia, Russia and England (I love Nyetember in particular).

Champagne and sparkling wines are, of course, a classic aperitif, but can also go well with food. Dry sparkling wine can work with spicy food and with some fish and chicken dishes, even fried food too. Ever tried a glass of bubbly with your fish and chips? Divine!!

Do note that contrary to wine, champagne labelled 'dry' is actually fruity and sweet while 'brut' is very dry. Remember, too, that the cooler the bottle, the less it will fizz on opening, so chill it well unless you want to spray everyone in the room.

Sherry After decades of relegation as old ladies' tipple, sherry is now one of the trendiest drinks, and deservedly so. This means many wonderful varieties are now becoming available outside of Spain. The range of sherries is vast – throw out your preconceptions!

Sherry is made in and around Jerez in Andalucia. It is a fortified wine, which means that it has added alcohol, typically brandy. Sherry also has a complicated fermentation process which varies from type to type. It should be noted that all natural sherries are dry; any sweetness is applied later. It is usually served in small, narrow wine glasses.

These are some of the main varieties of sherry that you might like to try:

Fino Fino means 'fine' in Spanish. It is the palest and the driest sherry, resembling a typical white wine in colour. Fino sherry is best served chilled as an aperitif and served with tapas or with olives and nuts.

Manzanilla This is a variety of fino. It is also dry but has a slightly salty flavour. Serve as you would fino.

Amontillado This starts life as a fino but then undergoes a different fermentation process. It is darker in colour and richer in flavour and should be served slightly chilled. Amontillado is also good as an aperitif or with light meats such as chicken.

Oloroso, meaning 'scented' in Spanish, is darker still than Amontillado. It is a wonderful, nutty sherry and comes either seco (dry) or dulce (sweet). Serve dry at room temperature, and it can accompany meats. Dulce should be served cold after a meal or with dessert.

Pedro Ximénez is exceptionally dark, almost black, intensely sweet and thick sherry made from pressed raisins. It is served cold, often as a pudding in itself.

Cream This is what most people associate with sherry. It is a blend of the main types of sherry from dry to sweet, and the result exported directly out of the country and not consumed by locals.

Dessert wine Dessert wines, also known as 'sticky' wines, are potent and full of flavour. They range from slightly sweet to very sweet, and thus are generally served with or as desserts in tiny glasses.

Sweet wines come in whites or reds, though the whites such as Moscatel, Sauternes, Barsac, and Tokaj are more typical. The reds are also wonderful, and are particularly good with chocolate or with berries. Like normal red and white wines, white dessert wine is served chilled and red served at room temperature or just slightly chilled. As a general rule, a dessert wine should always be sweeter than the dessert it accompanies.

Wines such as Vin Santo from Italy are made from grapes that have been partially dried after harvesting. Botrytised wines are made from grapes infected by the mold *Botrytis cinerea*, also known as noble rot! These include Sauternes, Tokaji Aszú, Beerenauslese and numerous wines from the Loire such as Quarts de Chaume. The wonderfully named Eiswein (ice wine) is made from grapes that are harvested while they are frozen.

Fortified wines Fortified wines are often sweeter than dessert wines and have a higher alcoholic content. Fortified wines have their fermentation process stopped by either the addition of a spirit, such as brandy, or have additional spirit added after fermentation. Examples include port, sherry, Madeira, vermouth and Marsala.

Don't forget, wine appreciation really is all a matter of taste, experimentation and asking the right questions. One last note, however – when using wine in the kitchen, never cook with a wine you wouldn't very happily drink!

Champagne Dover Sole with Clams and Julienne of Vegetables

If you want fish for a special occasion, head straight for Dover sole, also known as black sole (see the photograph on page 95). It is quite an expensive fish due to the fact that it only lives in European waters so cannot be widely caught throughout the world. This is an incredibly delicious fish, and if you're going to splash out on it for a celebration, it seems fitting to serve it with champagne sauce! If you still want to make this dish but can't find Dover sole, use other good-quality white fish such as turbot, brill, plaice or lemon sole.

1 Preheat the oven to 180°C (350°F), Gas mark 4.

2 Prepare each fish by removing the head, if you wish, and washing the fish well. Lay on a chopping board, white skin side down and with the tail end pointing towards you. Starting at the middle of the tail end, use a sharp knife to cut as neatly as possible through the skin (but not all the way through to the other side) right around the outer edge of the fish, just where the fringe meets the flesh. Finish off back at the tail end so that where you began the cut and where you end the cut cross over each other in an 'X' at the tail (see the drawing on page 95). This will create a 'flap', which you will be able peel open once the fish is cooked, revealing the flesh underneath. Prepare each fish in this way.

3 Pour 60ml (2fl oz) of water into two roasting tins (you might fit two fish per tray), which will create steam in the oven to cook the fish. Lay the fish in a single layer (cut side up) on the roasting tins. Sprinkle with salt and pepper and bake in the oven for 15 minutes (for a small fish) to 25 minutes (for an average sized sole). If you are cooking a large fish, such as brill or turbot, you may need to cook it for as much as 35 minutes. The fish is cooked when the skin lifts easily off the flesh from the tail end (where your 'X' meets), and the flesh should be opaque white with no trace of pink. When the fish

SERVES 4

4 fresh Dover sole, on the bone
Salt and freshly ground
  black pepper

**FOR THE CHAMPAGNE SAUCE
WITH CLAMS**

175ml (6fl oz) champagne
  or dry sparkling white wine
  (it can be a leftover half-
  drunk bottle!)
1 level tbsp chopped
  fresh shallot
2 large egg yolks
100g (4oz) butter, diced
24 clams in their shells,
  scrubbed clean – discard
  any that don't close when
  tapped
100ml (3½fl oz) double
  cream, lightly whipped

**FOR THE JULIENNE
OF VEGETABLES**

1 carrot, peeled
1 courgette (about 15cm/
  6in long)
½ cucumber, peeled if you
  wish (I normally don't)
15g (½oz) butter or 2 tbsp
  olive oil
salt and freshly ground
  black pepper

TO SERVE

4 wedges of lemon

is cooked it will sit quite happily in a warm oven (with the skin still attached) for up to 30 minutes.

4 To make the champagne sauce, first gently boil the champagne in a saucepan with the shallot until the mixture has reduced down to about 1 tablespoon. Take off the heat and allow it to cool for a minute. When you can hold your hands on the sides of the saucepan without them getting too hot, then you can go on. Place the saucepan on a very low heat and whisk in the egg yolks. Then whisk in the butter, two pieces at a time. If the pan gets too hot, take it off the heat for a few seconds or the sauce will scramble or split.

5 Place the clams with 30ml (1fl oz) water in a shallow, wide saucepan, cover with a lid and place on a low to medium heat until the clams open, about 4 minutes. Remove the clams and reserve the liquid left in the pan if there is any. Take the clams out of the shells and add to the warm champagne sauce; they will keep warm in the sauce. Pour any reserved liquid through a sieve and add a little of it (1 or 2 tablespoons) to the sauce to give a subtle flavour and also to thin the sauce.

6 To prepare the julienne of vegetables, use the coarsest part of your grater to grate the carrot and set aside in a bowl. Into another bowl, coarsely grate the courgette and cucumber lengthways, but do not grate the seeds – discard the watery seeds.

7 When you are ready to serve, heat a frying pan, add the butter or olive oil and, when hot, add the carrot and cook for 30 seconds. Then add the courgette and cucumber and continue to cook on a high heat for another 1 or 2 minutes until the vegetables are just softened. Season to taste. Fold the whipped cream into the warm champagne sauce.

8 Place the fish on warmed serving plates. I like to serve it on the bone, but of course you can take it off the bone using a fish slice or palette knife. Drizzle generously with the champagne sauce with clams and serve with the julienne of vegetables and a lemon wedge.

Variation
If you'd prefer not to use clams, you can use the same quantity of small prawns or shrimps.

Carpaccio of Fish with Peppers and Fresh Herbs

The technique used in this recipe is usually more associated with preparing and serving finely sliced uncooked beef. This is such a wonderful and unusual recipe, and is an elegant way to begin a special meal.

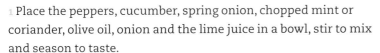

1 Place the peppers, cucumber, spring onion, chopped mint or coriander, olive oil, onion and the lime juice in a bowl, stir to mix and season to taste.

2 If the fish fillets are on the fat side, slice them thinly. Brush the fillets with a teaspoon of oil on each side. Place the fillets, one piece at a time, between two sheets of cling film and bash with a rolling pin until 2–3mm (1/8in) thick and about the size of the centre of a serving plate. This makes the fish very thin and also breaks down the tough sinew in the fish to make it wonderfully tender. Cover with cling film and keep in the fridge until ready to serve.

3 To serve, drizzle the sauce over the fish and scatter the mint or coriander leaves.

Rachel's handy tip

If you don't want to serve raw fish, you could either use smoked salmon or brush extra lemon or lime juice over the fish and leave in the fridge for at least 30 minutes before serving. The acids in the juice will cure or 'cook' the fish.

SERVES 4 AS A STARTER
OR LIGHT LUNCH

1/2 each small green, red and yellow pepper, deseeded and cut into 5mm (1/4in) pieces

4cm (11/4in) piece of cucumber, thinly sliced

1 spring onion, trimmed and finely sliced at an angle

1 generous tbsp chopped fresh mint or coriander

2 tbsp olive oil

1 tbsp snipped chives or 1/4 red onion, peeled and finely sliced

Juice of 1/2 lime

Salt and freshly ground black pepper

300g (11oz) fish fillets, such as salmon, tuna, monkfish, sole or plaice

1 tbsp sunflower oil

TO SERVE
Chopped mint or whole coriander leaves

Fillet Steak with Mushroom and Brandy Sauce and Tomato Fondue

SERVES 4

FOR THE MUSHROOM AND BRANDY SAUCE
50g (2oz) butter
400g (14oz) mushrooms, wiped and sliced
90ml (3fl oz) brandy
225ml (8fl oz) chicken or light beef stock
175ml (6fl oz) single cream
1 tbsp chopped fresh thyme
Salt and freshly ground black pepper

FOR THE TOMATO FONDUE
3 tbsp olive oil
1 onion, peeled and sliced
1 clove of garlic, peeled and crushed
2 x 400g tins chopped tomatoes or use 900g (2lb) fresh tomatoes, peeled and chopped (see handy tip on page 26)
1 tbsp chopped fresh herbs, such as basil, parsley, marjoram or tarragon
Sea salt, freshly ground black pepper and sugar

4 x 175g (6oz) fillet steak
A little olive oil

Fillet steak, also known as filet mignon or beef tenderloin, is the tenderest cut of beef you can buy and, as a result, one of the most expensive. This means it is certainly best saved for important meals, and when you taste it you will certainly understand why! You can decide how rare or well done you prefer it to be, but it is considered at its very best when served rare.

1 First make the mushroom and brandy sauce. Heat the butter on a high heat in a medium-sized frying pan. Add the mushrooms and sauté for 7–9 minutes until deep golden brown. Measure the brandy into a small bowl and add quickly to the mushrooms. Allow to boil, but stand back as it might flame. Add the stock and allow it to boil, and then add the cream. Boil the mixture for 4–5 minutes until it has thickened and finally add the thyme leaves and season to taste.
2 Then make the tomato fondue. Heat the oil in a medium-sized saucepan. Add the onion and garlic, toss until coated, then cover and sweat over a gentle heat until soft and a tiny bit golden. Add the tomatoes and chopped herbs, mix and season with salt and pepper and a pinch of sugar. Gently simmer, uncovered, for approximately 30 minutes or until softened.
3 When you are ready to eat, heat up a grill pan or a heavy, large frying pan for cooking the steaks. Drizzle the steaks with olive oil and sea salt and pepper. Place the steaks on the hot pan and cook on either side for a few minutes if you want it rare, approximately 6 minutes for medium rare or 8–10 minutes for well done. When the steaks are cooked, take them off the pan, allow them to rest for 2 minutes then serve each with a lovely helping of mushroom and brandy sauce and the tomato fondue.

Rachel's handy tip

If you are worried about flaming the brandy, add the stock at the same time. However, if the flames do get out of control, cover with a fire blanket – never add water.

The Lazy Sunday

One of life's greatest pleasures is a relaxed Sunday spent at home, sharing long breakfasts, lingering over the papers, making wonderful food and going for leisurely walks. This is your time to spend however you please, but it's also the perfect opportunity to gather friends and family around the table. Make the most of your lazy day – there's no need to rush and you can even keep your slippers on!

Freshly Squeezed Juices

EACH MAKES 4 GLASSES
VEGETARIAN

**RASPBERRY AND
ORANGE JUICE**
Juice of 6 oranges
125g (4½oz) raspberries

PEACH AND RASPBERRY JUICE
8 peaches
125g (4½oz) raspberries

MANGO AND APPLE JUICE
1 mango, peeled and
  stone removed
8 apples, cut into quarters

**BLACKBERRY AND
APPLE JUICE**
125g (4½oz) blackberries
8 apples, cut into quarters

**CRANBERRY AND
APPLE JUICE**
75g (3oz) raw cranberries
8 apples, cut into quarters

**APPLE, BANANA AND
STRAWBERRY SMOOTHIE**
6 apples, cut into quarters
2 bananas
225g (8oz) strawberries

**MELON AND STRAWBERRY
JUICE**
1 charentais, ogen, galia,
  canteloupe, watermelon
  or honeydew melon, skin
  removed and flesh chopped
225g (8oz) strawberries

It's Sunday and you have time to indulge, so go ahead and treat yourself to freshly squeezed juice. These are zingy breakfast juices, but if you're having guests for brunch, try the raspberry and orange juice mixed with champagne, cava, prosecco or sparkling wine.

Raspberry and orange juice
Place the orange juice and raspberries in a liquidiser and whiz, then push through a sieve. Serve immediately.

Peach and raspberry juice
Stone the peaches and run through a juicer with the raspberries, or liquidise and push through a sieve. Serve immediately.

Mango and apple juice
Place the mango flesh in a juicer followed by the apples and whiz, or liquidise and push through a sieve. Serve immediately.

Blackberry and apple juice
Whiz the blackberries followed by the apples in a juicer, or liquidise and push through a sieve. Serve immediately.

Cranberry and apple juice
For a great punchy juice, run the cranberries through the juicer followed by the apples, or liquidise and push through a sieve. Serve immediately.

Apple, banana and strawberry smoothie
Juice the apples, then put the juice, banana and strawberries in a blender and whiz. Or, peel and core the apples and liquidise with the other ingredients and push through a sieve. Serve immediately.

Melon and strawberry juice
Place the chopped melon and strawberries in a juicer and whiz, or liquidise and push through a sieve. Serve immediately.

Baked Eggs with Chorizo, Cream and Cheese

This is one of my favourite breakfast or brunch recipes. In fact, it would also be good for supper too! It's the perfect start to a long and lazy Sunday.

. ─────────── · ☆ · ─────────── .

1 Preheat the oven to 230°C (450°F), Gas mark 8.

2 Mix the tomato purée (if using) with the cream and season with salt, pepper and a pinch of sugar. Spoon half of the cream mixture into the base of two ovenproof cups, bowls or ramekins. Add two slices of chorizo to each dish, then crack two eggs into each dish, and top with the remaining three slices of chorizo each. Spoon over the remaining tomato cream, then sprinkle with the grated cheese.

3 Place in the hot oven and cook for 9–12 minutes, or until the whites are set. Serve on their own or with buttered toast.

SERVES 4

2 tsp tomato purée (optional)
4 tbsp double cream
Salt, freshly ground black
    pepper and sugar
16 thin slices of chorizo,
    2cm (¾in) in diameter
8 eggs
2 generous tbsp grated cheese,
    such as Gruyère or Cheddar

Blueberry and Almond Muffins

MAKES 10 MUFFINS
VEGETARIAN

200g (7oz) plain flour
1 generous tsp baking powder
1 level tsp ground mixed spice
50g (2oz) ground almonds
175g (6oz) sugar
200ml (7fl oz) buttermilk
1 egg
50g (2oz) butter, melted
100g (4oz) blueberries
2 tbsp nibbed (chopped)
   almonds (optional)

Muffins are such a homely breakfast treat, and the warm smells permeating the house are a gentle way to wake the family. You can even make the batter the night before so you can have a few extra minutes in bed the next morning.

1 Preheat the oven to 200°C (400°F), Gas mark 6. Line a muffin tray with 10 paper muffin cases.

2 Sift the flour, baking powder and mixed spice into a large bowl, add the ground almonds and sugar. Place the buttermilk, egg and melted butter in another medium-sized bowl and beat together. Add to the dry ingredients and mix to make a smooth batter. Fold in the blueberries.

3 Divide the mixture between the 10 muffin cases, filling them three-quarters full. Scatter over the nibbed almonds, if using, and bake in the oven for about 20 minutes, until golden and firm to the touch in the centre. Remove from the oven when cooked and allow to cool slightly in the tray and then transfer to a wire rack.

The Big Sunday Roast

Sunday roasts are such a great ritual. They do take time and preparation, but the real joy is in being able to spend the day in the kitchen with family and friends gathered around. I often hear people say they're intimidated by making a big roast because they're concerned they won't have all the food ready at the same time. If you follow the chart below, you should have no problem. Some ovens are hotter than others, so you may find you need to try this a couple of times to tweak your cooking times accordingly. This chart presumes you will be making the following recipes to serve together:

❀ Mum's Roast Chicken with Lemony Breadcrumb Stuffing and Gravy (opposite)

❀ Sautéed Buttered Cabbage (see page 113)

❀ Root Vegetable Mash (see page 113)

❀ Granny's Roast Herbed Potatoes (see page 114)

❀ Glazed Carrots with Herbs (see page 115).

Planning your feast
These times are working on the assumption that you will sit down to eat at 1pm.

Dish	Length of cooking time	Begin preparation	Dish in oven/ on hob	Dish ready
Stuffing	10 minutes	10.15am	—	—
Roast chicken	2 hours	10.30am	10.45am	12.45pm, allowing 15 minutes to rest the chicken
Root vegetable mash	20 minutes	10.45am	11am	11.20am, reheat when ready to eat
Have a cup of tea!!	2 minutes	11am	—	11.02am, drink immediately
Roast herbed potatoes	35–55 minutes	11.45am	12 noon	12.50pm, keep warm in oven, uncovered
Glazed carrots with herbs	20 minutes	12 noon	12.25pm	12.45pm, keep warm in oven
Gravy	5 minutes	—	12.45pm	12.50pm, keep warm in oven
Buttered cabbage	2–3 minutes	12.15am	12.50pm	12.55pm, serve immediately

Mum's Roast Chicken with Lemony Breadcrumb Stuffing and Gravy

I often yearn for my mum's roast chicken (see the photograph overleaf) with her delicious lemony stuffing – there's simply nothing else like it.

1 Preheat the oven to 180°C (350°F), Gas mark 4.

2 First, make the stuffing. Melt the butter in a saucepan and add the onion. Cover and cook over a low heat for 8–10 minutes, until the onion is soft (see the handy tip on page 15). Take off the heat, then stir in the chopped herbs, lemon zest, lemon juice and breadcrumbs. Season to taste.

3 Spoon the stuffing into the chicken carcass and place the chicken in a roasting tray. Smear the knob of soft butter over the skin and sprinkle with some sea salt and pepper. Roast for 1 1/2–1 3/4 hours, until cooked. The legs should feel quite loose in the bird and when a skewer is stuck into the thigh with a spoon placed underneath to catch the juices, the juices should run clear. If it begins to look quite dark while cooking, cover with some foil or parchment paper. When cooked, transfer the chicken to a serving plate and leave to rest, in a warm oven if possible, while you make the gravy.

4 Place the roasting tray directly on the hob on a medium heat, add half the stock and bring to the boil, whisking to release the sweet juicy bits that have stuck to the tray (this is called deglazing). When it comes to the boil, pour into a mais-gras, or a small bowl or heatproof glass jug. If using a bowl/jug, degrease the juices by adding one or two ice-cubes – these will draw the fat up to the top, so you can spoon it off and discard. If using a mais-gras, degrease the juices in the usual way.

5 Pour the degreased juices into a small saucepan, add the remainder of the stock, bring to the boil, and season to taste. If it's a little watery, boil for another couple of minutes.

6 Take the chicken out of the oven and carve when ready to serve.

Rachel's handy tips

To make breadcrumbs, place slices of white bread (with or without the crusts) in a food processor, and whiz until you have crumbs, about 20 seconds. Mum usually chops her onions and parsley, separately, in the food processor for the stuffing too.

MUM'S ROAST CHICKEN
WITH LEMONY BREADCRUMB
STUFFING AND GRAVY
SERVES 4–6
1 large chicken, 1.5–2.25kg
   (3lb 5oz–5lb)
A small knob of butter
Sea salt and freshly ground
   black pepper
350ml (12fl oz) chicken
   stock for the gravy

FOR THE STUFFING
25g (1oz) butter
1 onion, peeled and chopped
2 tbsp chopped fresh parsley
1 tsp chopped fresh thyme
1 tsp chopped fresh sage
Finely grated zest of 1 lemon
Juice of 1/2 a lemon
100g (4oz) soft breadcrumbs

Sautéed Buttered Cabbage

This is the way we prepare cabbage at the cookery school (it is also included in the photograph on the previous page). Because it's not boiled, it retains its flavour and goodness.

1 Remove the tough outer leaves from the cabbage. Cut the head of cabbage into four, from top to bottom. Cut out the core, then slice the cabbage crossways into fine shreds, about 5mm (1/4in) thick.
2 Place the butter and water in a wide saucepan on a medium heat, allow the butter to melt and then toss in the cabbage. Season with salt and pepper. Cover with a lid and cook on the heat (not allowing the cabbage to burn) for 2–3 minutes until just softened. Taste immediately for seasoning and serve.

Variations
For some added spice, add 1/2 teaspoon of ground caraway seeds and a pinch of chilli flakes to the cabbage when it's cooking.

Root Vegetable Mash

You could serve traditional mashed potatoes with a Sunday roast, but this is a delicious and sweet variation which really complements roast meat.

1 Peel the vegetables and chop into 2cm (3/4in) dice, keeping the swede and carrot separate from the other vegetables.
2 Place the chopped swede and carrot in a large saucepan, cover with cold water, add a pinch of salt and boil for 5 minutes, then add the parsnip, celeriac and sweet potato and continue boiling for another 15 minutes or until all the vegetables are cooked.
3 Drain very well, then add the butter (or olive oil) and the cream, if using. Mash rustically by hand or, if you want a smoother mash, use a food processor. Season to taste and add the chopped herbs. This can be made in advance and reheated when you are ready to eat.

Variations
If you feel like a change, drizzle some pesto sauce or scatter some toasted pine nuts over the mash just before serving.

SAUTÉED BUTTERED
CABBAGE
SERVES 4–6
VEGETARIAN
450g (1lb) Savoy cabbage
    (or another dark green,
    leafy cabbage)
25g (1oz) butter
2 tbsp water
Salt and freshly ground
    black pepper

ROOT VEGETABLE MASH
SERVES 4–6
VEGETARIAN
1/4–1/2 swede
1 carrot
1 parsnip
1/2 celeriac
1 small sweet potato
15g (1/2oz) butter or 2 tbsp
    olive oil
30ml (1fl oz) single or double
    cream (optional)
Salt and freshly ground
    black pepper
1 tbsp chopped fresh parsley

8–10 large floury potatoes,
   peeled and, if large,
   cut in half
Olive oil, duck or goose fat,
   or beef dripping
Sea salt
4 sprigs of fresh thyme or
   2 sprigs of rosemary

Granny's Roast Herbed Potatoes

Some roast meats, like beef or traditional stuffed chicken, simply demand really good, roast potatoes as an accompaniment . My grandmother makes the best roast potatoes, the ones that are crispy and crunchy on the outside, and soft on the inside. The trick is to parboil the potatoes, then drain them and shake them in the saucepan before roasting.

1 Preheat the oven to 220°C (425°F), Gas mark 7.

2 Drop the potatoes into boiling salted water and cook for 10 minutes. Drain off the water and shake the potatoes around in the dry saucepan with the lid on – this roughens the surface of the potatoes and make them crispier.

3 Heat a few tablespoons of olive oil (or duck, goose or beef fat) in a roasting tray on the hob and toss the potatoes in it, making sure they are well coated (add more fat if they are not). Sprinkle with salt and place in the hot oven for 35–55 minutes, basting (spooning the hot oil of fat over them) every now and then and turning over after 20 minutes or so.

4 When they are nearly cooked, add in the whole herb sprigs, tucked in between the potatoes. You can turn the oven down to 200°C (400°F), Gas mark 6 after 15–20 minutes if you think they are dark enough. If the potatoes have to keep warm in the oven for any amount of time, do not cover them or they will go soggy.

Glazed Carrots with Herbs

This method of cooking carrots takes only a tad more concentration then boiling carrots, but the difference in flavour is immense. The carrots are cooked with just a small amount of butter and a drop of water so they keep all their flavour and goodness. When we show the students at the cookery school how to cook carrots like this, they are always so pleasantly surprised with the end result. For a photograph of both the carrots and root vegetables, see page 110.

1 Cut the carrots into 5mm (1/4in) thick slices, either straight across or at an angle, making sure they are as even as possible so they all cook at the same rate. Leave baby carrots whole.
2 Place the carrots, butter, water, salt and pepper in a medium-sized saucepan on a medium heat. Bring to the boil, cover with a lid and cook over a gentle heat for 15–20 minutes until tender. By this point the liquid should have all been absorbed into the carrots and created a glaze, but if there is still liquid in the pan when the carrots are almost cooked, remove the lid and boil until any remaining liquid has evaporated (don't burn!) and the carrots are glazed. Add the chopped herbs, season and serve.

Rachel's handy tips

⚜ If you are making the glazed carrots ahead of time, cover them and keep warm. Add the chopped herbs just before serving.
⚜ The herbs I add to the carrots depend on what I'm serving them with. To accompany a lamb roast I would add mint, parsley, tarragon or marjoram, but if serving with slow roast of lamb with spices, I would add chopped coriander.

GLAZED CARROTS
WITH HERBS
SERVES 4–6
VEGETARIAN
450g (1lb) carrots, topped, tailed and cleaned (peel if they need it or are not organic)
15g (1/2oz) butter
125ml (4fl oz) water
Pinch of salt and freshly ground black pepper
1–2 tbsp chopped fresh mint, parsley, tarragon, marjoram or coriander

Slow Roast Chicken with Lemon and Chilli

SERVES 4–6

1 large chicken, 1.5–2.25kg
(3lb 5oz–5lb)
4 cloves of garlic, peeled and
crushed or grated
1 red chilli, deseeded and
finely chopped
2 tsp paprika
1 tsp salt
Juice of 1 lemon (about
60ml/2fl oz)
2 tbsp olive oil
Sea salt for sprinkling on
the chicken

FOR THE GRAVY

300ml (½ pint) chicken stock
Squeeze of lemon juice
Salt and freshly ground
black pepper

This is another great way of cooking roast chicken (although if you're cooking it for Sunday lunch as in the previous recipe, please note the time will vary from the chart). I adore the fresh flavours of this recipe. It's great served hot in the winter with roast potatoes and delicious vegetables such as Honey Roast Parsnips (see page 118) or Broccoli with Garlic, Lemon and Parmesan (see page 118). In the summertime, serve it at almost room temperature with couscous or a big salad.

1 Preheat the oven to 160°C (325°F), Gas mark 3.
2 Using sharp kitchen scissors, cut along both sides of the backbone and discard the backbone (or put it into your stockpot). Place the chicken on a roasting tray, skin side up and, using your hand, press down on the breastbone to flatten the chicken.
3 In a small bowl, mix together the garlic, chilli, paprika, salt, lemon juice and olive oil. Using the point of a sharp knife or skewer, make deep holes all over the chicken. Spoon or pour the flavoured oil all over the chicken, making sure it gets into every crevice. Sprinkle with sea salt.
4 Roast in the oven for 2 hours, basting every now and then, until the chicken is tender and completely cooked. Transfer the chicken to a serving plate and leave it to rest in a warm place, while you turn your mind to the gravy.
5 To make the gravy, follow steps 4 and 5 on page 109, but adding the lemon juice together with the seasoning.
6 Carve the chicken and serve with the gravy and the vegetables of your choice.

Rachel's handy tip

If I'm serving this at room temperature with a salad, I prefer not to make a gravy. Instead, degrease the juices (see step 4 on page 109), add the lemon juice and pour the sauce over the chicken on a large serving plate.

Honey Roast Parsnips with Sesame Seeds

SERVES 4–6
VEGETARIAN
500g (1lb 2oz) parsnips (4 large or 6 medium), peeled
2 tbsp honey
Sea salt
2 tbsp olive oil
2 tbsp sesame seeds

These are so lovely and sticky, and make a great variation to traditional roast parsnips (see the photograph on page 117).

1 Preheat the oven to 230°C (450°F), Gas mark 8.
2 Quarter the parsnips and remove the woody central root. Slice into long, even chunks, about 6cm (2½in) long and 1cm (½in) wide. Place in a saucepan of boiling water on the heat and boil for 3 minutes. Drain and dry on kitchen paper. Toss in a bowl with the honey and a good pinch of sea salt. Drizzle the olive oil over, toss and empty out onto a roasting tray. Place in the oven and roast for 15–20 minutes, until golden brown and soft.
3 While the parsnips are cooking, place the sesame seeds in a dry frying pan on a medium heat. Toss for about a minute, until the seeds turn a golden brown. When the parsnips are cooked, transfer them to a warm serving bowl, and sprinkle with the sesame seeds.

Broccoli with Garlic, Lemon and Parmesan

SERVES 10–15
VEGETARIAN
2 large heads of broccoli
1 tsp salt
4 tbsp olive oil
4 cloves of garlic, peeled and crushed or grated
Finely grated zest of 1 large lemon
Sea salt and freshly ground black pepper
75g (3oz) Parmesan cheese, grated (optional)

I love this way of cooking broccoli (see also the photograph on page 117), and I sometimes add a red deseeded chilli to the mix as well.

1 Peel off the tough outer parts of the broccoli stems and cut the florets into long thin stalks. If they are large, cut in half lengthways.
2 Add the salt to a saucepan of water and bring to the boil, add the broccoli and cook on a high heat with the lid off for about 5–6 minutes until cooked. Drain the broccoli and set aside.
3 Pour the olive oil into a frying pan on a high heat, add the garlic and cook for a minute until pale golden, then add the broccoli and lemon zest and season with salt and pepper. Transfer to a warm serving bowl, sprinkle with the grated Parmesan and serve.

Slow Roast Spiced Lamb with Roasted Root Vegetables

Shoulder of lamb responds very well to slow roasting. The long cooking time at a low heat makes the meat deliciously succulent, and all the fat renders out so the skin becomes crisp and delicious. The lamb needs very little attention for the four hours it's in the oven (just a little basting every now and then), making it the perfect dish for a lazy Sunday (see the photograph on page 120). I like to cook the lamb on the bone to give it more flavour. The meat is so tender it comes off in chunks, rather than thin slices, which makes carving very easy. The spices used to flavour the lamb go so well with the sweet roasted vegetables. A shoulder can vary in size depending on the age of the lamb. Early lamb will serve 6–8, but a late lamb (also know as hogget) is best for slow roasting and will serve 12–15 people.

1 Preheat the oven to 220°C (425°F), Gas mark 7.

2 Using a very sharp knife, make long but shallow incisions into the shoulder of lamb all over the skin.

3 In a small bowl mix the ground cumin and coriander with a few good pinches of sea salt, pepper and the olive oil. Spread this spicy oil over the lamb, rubbing it in with your fingers, then place the lamb skin-side up on a roasting tray. Sprinkle the skin with salt.

4 Place in the oven for 20 minutes, then turn the heat down to 160°C (325°F), Gas mark 3 and roast for 4 hours. Baste it every 15 minutes or so by spooning the juices over the meat. The cooking time will, of course, depend on the size of the shoulder, but when it's cooked the meat will be very tender and almost falling off the bone in the most gorgeous way.

5 About 20 minutes before the meat is due to come out of the oven, peel the vegetables and cut into 2cm (3/4in) cubes. Dry the cut vegetables with kitchen paper, then put them in a bowl and toss with olive oil and season with salt and pepper. The vegetables should all be coated with a thin layer of olive oil; if you have extra vegetables, add more olive oil.

6 Spread them out in a single layer on one or two roasting trays and

SERVES 10–15

FOR THE SHOULDER OF LAMB
1 shoulder of lamb, weighing approx 3kg (6lb 10oz)
2 tbsp cumin seeds, toasted and ground (see handy tip)
2 tbsp coriander seeds, toasted and ground
Sea salt and freshly ground black pepper
60ml (2fl oz) olive oil
900ml (1½ pints) lamb or chicken stock, for the gravy

FOR THE YOGHURT AND CUCUMBER RAITA
500ml (18fl oz) Greek or plain natural yoghurt
1 small cucumber, seeded and finely diced
2 tomatoes, diced
4 cloves of garlic, peeled and crushed or grated
3 tbsp chopped fresh coriander or mint
Finely grated zest and juice of 1 lime
Salt and freshly ground black pepper

FOR THE ROASTED ROOT VEGETABLES
2 parsnips
2 carrots
1 celeriac
1 swede
1 large sweet potato
60–75ml (2–2½fl oz) olive oil
Sea salt and freshly ground black pepper

cook in the oven for 25–35 minutes or until golden on the outside and soft on the inside. Do not try to turn them while they are cooking as they will only lift off the tray when they are fully cooked.

7 When the lamb is ready, transfer the meat to a serving platter, cover and keep warm while you make the gravy.

8 To make the gravy, place the roasting tray on the hob on a medium heat, add half the stock and bring to the boil, whisking to release the sweet juicy bits that have stuck to the tray (this is called deglazing). When it comes to the boil, pour it into a mais-gras, or a small bowl or heatproof jug. If using a bowl/jug add one or two ice-cubes to draw the fat up to the top, then you can spoon the fat off and discard. If using a mais-gras, degrease the juices in the usual way. Pour the degreased juices into a small saucepan, add the remainder of the stock, bring to the boil, and season to taste. If it's a little watery, boil it for another couple of minutes.

9 To make the raita, put the yoghurt into a bowl, add the cucumber, garlic, herbs, lime zest and juice and some salt and pepper to taste. Stir together and refrigerate until ready.

10 To serve, cut the meat into slices, pour over the gravy and spoon on the roast vegetables and the raita for dipping into.

Rachel's handy tips

To toast spice seeds, fry them in a dry, un-oiled pan for 30 seconds over a medium-high heat until deeper in colour and smelling fragrant (keep moving them around).

Because this lamb is so tender, if I have any left over, I reheat it in an ovenproof dish covered in gravy so that the meat doesn't dry out.

An Elegant Afternoon

A proper afternoon tea is a great excuse to invite your best friends around for a good gossip and to serve all the pretty, frilly, girly food that you might not otherwise have the opportunity to make. It's such a lovely way to spend the afternoon. The care you put into the presentation is sure to put a smile on everyone's faces! So dig out your cake stands and put on your favourite dress and watch your worries disappear.

Sweet Scones with Blueberry Jam

MAKES 10 MEDIUM SCONES
VEGETARIAN

FOR THE JAM
Makes 2 small jars of jam
375g (15oz) blueberries,
    fresh or frozen
30ml (1fl oz) water
300g (11oz) sugar
3 tbsp lemon juice

FOR THE SCONES
450g (1lb) plain flour
Pinch of salt
20g (3/4oz) baking powder
25g (1oz) caster sugar
75g (3oz) butter
2 eggs
200ml (7fl oz) milk
75g (3oz) raisins or sultanas
    (optional)

FOR A CRUNCHY GLAZE
(OPTIONAL)
1 small egg, beaten (if there
    is no liquid left from
    the scones)
Granulated sugar

Afternoon tea just wouldn't be right without scones! They are so simple and delicious, particularly with homemade jam, which is much easier to make than many people realise. This scone recipe comes from Elizabeth O'Connell, Isaac's maternal grandmother.

1 First make the jam, which will then keep in a cool place for several months. Place a saucer in the fridge for testing the jam later. To sterilise the jars (any shape will do, preferably with a lid), put them through a dishwasher cycle, boil in a pan of water for 5 minutes, or place in a preheated oven (150°C/300°F/Gas mark 2), for 10 minutes.
2 Place the blueberries and water in a medium-sized saucepan on a medium heat. Bring to the boil and mash the fruit with a potato masher. Add the sugar and lemon juice and stir over a high heat for 5 minutes. Test by placing a small blob on the chilled saucer, leave for 20 seconds and run your finger through the blob. If it forms a skin, the jam is set. Carefully remove the jars from the dishwasher, pan or oven, using oven gloves if necessary. Pour the jam into the jars immediately and cover with a lid or jam pot cover.
3 To make the scones, preheat the oven to 230°C (450°F), Gas mark 8.
4 Sieve the flour, salt and baking powder into a large bowl, add the caster sugar and mix. Rub in the butter and make a well in the centre. In another bowl, whisk the eggs and then add the milk. Pour all but 60ml (2fl oz) of this liquid into the dry ingredients and, using one hand, mix to a soft dough, adding more liquid if necessary.
5 Turn out onto a floured work surface and knead until a dough is formed. Sprinkle with flour and gently roll out until it's 2–5cm (3/4–2in) thick. Cut with a knife or a round 5cm (2in) cutter into scones. Place on a lightly floured baking tray.
6 If you opt for a crunchy glaze, brush the scones with the liquid left in the bowl or with a beaten egg, then dip each one, wet side down, into the granulated sugar. Return to the baking tray, sugared side up.
7 Bake in the centre of the oven for 7–10 minutes until golden brown on top. Cool on a wire rack. Serve split with butter and jam or with jam and a blob of whipped cream or clotted cream.

Iced Vanilla Cup Cakes

These pretty little cup cakes come out of the oven flat on top. For extra decoration, top them with a little crystallised flower, sugared almond or other edible decoration. The cakes are very light as the eggs are whisked for about 10 minutes until they are full of air and they only use a tiny quantity of butter.

1 Preheat the oven to 200°C (400°F), Gas mark 6. Place 12 paper bun cases in a bun tray.
2 Heat the milk in a saucepan until it almost comes to the boil, take it off the heat, add the butter and stir to melt, then set aside.
3 Sift the flour with the baking powder, add the salt. In a separate large bowl, beat the eggs and vanilla extract with an electric hand mixer until light and fluffy, about 10 minutes. Gradually beat in the sugar until thick and mousse-like. Turn the speed down and blend in the flour, then the milk. Stop beating as soon as it's all mixed in.
4 Spoon into each paper case and bake in the oven for 15 minutes or until golden and firm to the touch. Allow to cool slightly in the tin before moving to a wire rack and icing.
5 To make the icing, mix the icing sugar with 1 tbsp cream and the vanilla extract; if it's not a good spreading consistency, add a little more cream. To ice the cupcakes, dip a table knife into boiling water and spread the icing over each cake with the warm knife.

MAKES 12 CUP CAKES
VEGETARIAN
75ml (2¹/₂fl oz) milk
Scant 25g (1oz) butter
75g (3oz) plain flour
¹/₂ tsp baking powder
Pinch of salt
2 medium eggs
1 tsp vanilla extract
125g (5oz) caster sugar

FOR THE ICING
100g (4oz) icing sugar, sifted
1–2 tbsp single cream
1 tsp vanilla extract

TO DECORATE
Crystallised flowers
Sugared almonds
Other edible decorations
 of your choice

Afternoon Tea Cake

MAKES 8 SLICES
VEGETARIAN

125g (5oz) mixture of dried
 fruit, such as raisins,
 sultanas, currants, chopped
 dates and chopped dried
 apricots
75ml (2½fl oz) Cointreau,
 brandy or whisky
200g (7oz) butter
150g (5oz) caster sugar
1 tbsp sunflower oil
3 eggs
250g (9oz) flour, sifted
1 tsp baking powder
Pinch of salt
Icing sugar, for dusting

I love this cake with its juicy mixture of fruit and just a hint of alcohol, and the bonus is that it's so easy to put together (see the photograph on page 126).

1 Preheat the oven to 180°C (350°F), Gas mark 4. Line the base of a 20cm (8in) cake tin with greaseproof paper and rub the sides with a butter wrapper to grease it.

2 Place the dried fruit and alcohol in a saucepan and bring to the boil. Let it simmer for a few seconds and then pour out into a bowl and allow to cool.

3 In a large bowl, beat the butter until soft, add the sugar and beat, then add the oil and the eggs one by one, beating all the time (I usually do this in a food mixer, but an electric hand mixer is just as good). Next, gently stir in the sifted flour, baking powder, salt, fruit and liqueur.

4 Transfer the cake batter into the prepared tin, smooth the top and cook in the oven for 50 minutes or until a skewer inserted into the cake centre comes out clean. Cool slightly before removing the cake from the tin and finish cooling on a wire rack. Dredge with icing sugar when cool.

White Chocolate Buns

For anyone like me who loves white chocolate, this is the perfect bun recipe (see the photograph on page 126). I find myself craving these when I really want something sweet and simple to go with my cup of tea.

(see the photograph on page 126)

1 Preheat the oven to 170°C (325°F), Gas mark 3 and line a bun tray with 12 paper bun cases.

2 In a medium-sized saucepan on a low heat melt the butter and then add 75g (3oz) of white chocolate and the caster sugar and stir until the chocolate has melted and the sugar dissolved. Stir to mix and set aside to cool for 2 minutes.

3 Meanwhile, sift the flour and baking powder into a large mixing bowl and add in the remaining chocolate. Beat the eggs in a separate small bowl. Add the beaten egg and vanilla extract to the chocolate mixture, stir to mix and then pour into the dry ingredients, folding it together. Pour the mixture into the bun cases and bake in the oven for 16–20 minutes minutes or until pale golden and just firm on top. Remove from the oven, take the buns out of the bun tray and leave to cool on a wire rack.

4 For the topping, melt the chocolate in a bowl sitting over a saucepan of simmering water (also known as a bain marie). Allow it to cool slightly until it's a little thicker, then, using a table knife or the back of a teaspoon, spread the melted chocolate over each cooled bun. Alternatively, drizzle the melted chocolate from a spoon in delicate patterns over the top. Allow the chocolate to set before serving.

Rachel's handy tip

These buns are so delicious and moist that, assuming you don't eat them all in one sitting, they will keep well in an airtight box for three or four days.

MAKES 12 BUNS
VEGETARIAN
75g (3oz) butter
125g (5oz) white chocolate, chopped
75g (3oz) caster sugar
150g (5oz) plain flour
½ tsp baking powder
2 eggs
½ tsp vanilla extract

FOR THE TOPPING
75g (3oz) white chocolate, chopped

Oaty Shortbread

MAKES ABOUT 40 BISCUITS
VEGETARIAN
275g (10oz) oats
100g (4oz) plain flour
150g (5oz) caster sugar
1/2 tsp bicarbonate of soda
1 level tsp salt
225g (8oz) butter, softened

These lovely biscuits are surprisingly delicate even though they contain hearty oats. They make a perfect afternoon treat.

1 Preheat the oven to 180°C (350°F), Gas mark 4.
2 Whiz the oats in a food processor until they are quite fine. Then add the remaining ingredients and whiz again until the dough comes together.
3 Roll out the dough on a floured work surface to a thickness of about 5mm (1/4in). Cut into squares, circles or shapes with biscuit cutters and place on baking trays (no need to grease or line).
4 Bake in the oven for 15–20 minutes or until pale golden and slightly firm. Remove from the oven and carefully transfer to a wire rack to cool. These will keep for five or six days in an airtight container, and they freeze well too.

Tea

How is it that this one very simple drink can be so soothing and relaxing yet simultaneously refreshing and exhilarating? I love the fact that everyone has their own way of making tea; it is a very personal thing. My father thinks my weak tea is ridiculous, but for me it is just perfect!

On average, we drink about three cups of tea a day. Most of us use the humble teabag, and though this is perfectly acceptable for everyday usage, if you want the finest and purest flavour you need to use loose tea leaves. The tea in bags is made from the leftover pieces (the 'dust') of tea leaves.

Many tea purists say that to make the perfect cuppa you must follow these directions. They may seem obvious, but real aficionados have this down to a fine art!

1 Always start with fresh water, not water that has been previously boiled or that has been sitting around in the kettle.
2 Warm the pot by swishing hot water around in it, then drain the pot before beginning to make your tea.
3 Measure the correct amount of tea into the pot. A standard guideline is 1 small teaspoon per cup of water, though this depends on your taste and the strength of the tea.
4 Next, pour the water onto the leaves in the pot. The water temperature required varies from tea to tea, but I have included guidelines below.
5 Allow the tea to steep to develop the flavour. Again, I have listed suggestions below for the different types of tea. If you don't steep the tea for long enough, it will not have the maximum flavour, but if you steep for too long, tannins will be released from the tea and it will taste too strong and bitter.
6 Finally, you need to separate the leaves from the liquid when the tea has steeped for the correct amount of time. I have a teapot with a little sieve basket inside which can be removed once the tea has steeped for long enough. You can also use a very inexpensive tea infuser, and simply straining the brewed tea away from the leaves works just as well!

Tea is claimed to have powerful health benefits, in part because of its antioxidant properties. Whether or not this is true, it is an undisputed fact that a soothing cup of tea can at least make us *feel* instantly better.

All tea comes from the same source: the *Camellia sinensis* tea bush. Whether a tea leaf

ends up in a cup of black, white, green or oolong tea depends entirely on what happens after it is picked. (Herbal and fruit teas are not true 'teas' but infusions or tisanes.)

Black tea is the most popular tea worldwide. It contains the most caffeine, but it does not have as many antioxidants as other types of tea. The surface areas of the picked leaves are rolled or crushed and then exposed to the open air until they have turned black and are fully oxidized, hence the name 'black tea'. Keemun, Assam, Darjeeling, the divinely smoky Lapsang Souchong and Ceylon are all examples of black tea, as is Earl Grey, which is scented with bergamot oil. Black tea should be made with water at a good rolling boil (100°C/212°F), and should be allowed to steep for about 4 minutes, with the exception of Darjeeling tea, which requires steeping for just 2 minutes.

White tea has the least amount of caffeine and the highest amount of antioxidants of the four main types of tea. It is the least processed and has a delicately sweet flavour.

White tea is made from the young new-growth buds before they have opened and which are still covered by fine white hair, which explains the higher price this tea commands. The buds are not oxidized at all, but just left to dry as is. While Chinese tea drinkers have known of white tea's health benefits since the Ming Dynasty, until recently it was virtually unknown outside of Asia. But not anymore – it is the tea of the moment. As with all teas, there are many varieties of white tea: White Peony, Silver Needle and White Cloud are just a few.

In order to protect the delicate fresh sweet flavour of white tea, it should be made with water that has only been heated to about

70°C/160°F, or when you see the first hint of steam. Only steep for about 2 minutes.

Green tea is closer to white tea than black as it is also non-oxidized. The difference between white and green tea is that green tea uses rolled leaves and not the buds. The grassy taste of green tea is quite similar to, but stronger than, that of white tea and is also lower in caffeine and higher in antioxidants than black tea. Gunpowder, Sencha and Hojicha are types of green tea.

Green teas should be made with water heated to around 82°C/180°F. The steam should be wafting or gently swirling out of the kettle, but not yet at a rolling boil. Green tea should typically steep for about 2–3 minutes.

Oolong tea (also known as wulong) is a traditional Chinese tea that falls between a black and a green as it is only partially oxidized. The leaves must only be bruised; if they were broken or crushed full oxidation would occur. Bruising tea for oolong usually occurs by throwing the leaves in baskets so only the edges of the leaves are opened up to the air. Pouchong and Formosa are two kinds of oolong tea.

Oolong tea should be made with water just below boiling, about 93°C/200°F. The water should be steaming rapidly and there should be many bubbles rising in the kettle, but not really breaking the surface. Allow the tea to steep for about 4 minutes.

There are times when a big cup of the basic black tea with milk works perfectly for me, especially first thing in the morning. Later on in the morning I love something a little different, such as Lapsang Souchong or Gunpowder Green Tea in a china cup. For an afternoon tea I find that nothing beats a cup of Earl Grey, and although I know tea connoisseurs would think this wrong, I love mine with a splash of milk! If I am feeling healthy and virtuous, I might have a cup of white tea, which is wonderfully high in antioxidants. So, whatever your favourite, be sure to relax and savour the moment!

Greek Almond Crescents

These are little macaroon-style biscuits, which keep very well.
They're great with tea or coffee, or even served with vanilla ice
cream at the end of a meal (see the photograph on page 136).

—————————— · ☕ · ——————————

1 Preheat the oven to 180°C (350°F), Gas mark 4 and line a baking
tray with parchment paper.

2 In a large bowl, mix together the ground almonds, caster sugar
and grated orange zest. In another medium-sized bowl, whisk the
egg whites for a few seconds until the whites are broken up. Pour
half of the egg white into the dry ingredients and mix until it comes
together – you may need to add more egg white, it should be quite
a soft and sticky mixture.

3 Roll the soft dough into a large sausage then divide it into
18 parts (each about 1 heaped teaspoon). Roll each piece in the
flaked almonds sprinkled on a plate and, with your hands, form
into simple crescent shapes. Place on the baking tray and cook
for 13–18 minutes until golden. Remove from the oven and cool
on a wire rack.

MAKES 18 CRESCENTS
VEGETARIAN
200g (7oz) ground almonds
100g (4oz) caster sugar
Finely grated zest of 1 orange
2 egg whites
50g (2oz) flaked almonds

Chocolate and Hazelnut Caramel Bars

This is a wickedly sweet and chocolatey tray bake. The recipe makes lots, so freeze some of the bars for another time if you wish.

——— · ☕ · ———

1 Preheat the oven to 160°C (325°F), Gas mark 3 and line the base or grease a small Swiss roll tin measuring 20 x 30cm (8 x 12in).

2 In a medium-sized saucepan over a medium heat, melt the butter for the chocolate base, stir in the cocoa powder and then the sugar and mix until smooth. Remove from the heat and stir in the eggs until mixed and then the plain flour. Spread the chocolate base over the prepared tin and bake in the oven for 20 minutes until firm on top. Remove from the oven and set aside to cool while you make the hazelnut caramel layer.

3 In a medium-sized saucepan and over a medium heat, melt the butter and then add the condensed milk, golden syrup and sugar. Turn the heat to low and stir continuously for 12–15 minutes until the mixture is dark caramel in colour – do not let it burn. Remove from the heat and stir in the nuts. Spread evenly over the chocolate base and allow to cool.

4 Meanwhile, melt the chocolate in a bowl sitting over a saucepan of simmering water (also known as a bain marie). When it is melted, stir in the oil and then pour over the caramel layer and smooth out, leaving to cool and set. Cut into squares. These will keep for a week in an airtight container.

MAKES 30 BARS
VEGETARIAN

FOR THE CHOCOLATE BASE
200g (7oz) butter
50g (2oz) cocoa powder
300g (11oz) caster sugar
2 eggs, beaten
225g (8oz) plain flour

FOR THE HAZELNUT CARAMEL LAYER
125g (4½oz) butter
1 x 397g tin of condensed milk
2 tbsp golden syrup
75g (3oz) caster sugar
125g (4½oz) toasted and halved hazelnuts

FOR THE CHOCOLATE TOPPING
200g (7oz) dark chocolate, chopped
1 tbsp sunflower or vegetable oil

Teatime Sandwiches

EACH FILLING MAKES 10–14
SMALL SANDWICHES

**SCRAMBLED EGGS
AND CHIVES**
2 eggs
1 tbsp milk
Salt and freshly ground
  black pepper
Small knob of butter
1/2 tbsp snipped fresh chives

**GOAT'S CHEESE AND
SUNDRIED TOMATOES**
125g (5oz) sundried tomatoes,
  chopped finely (I like semi-
  sundried or sun-blushed
  tomatoes)
75g (3oz) soft goat's cheese
1 tbsp chopped fresh basil or
  1 tsp chopped fresh thyme

TARRAGON CHICKEN
2 chicken breasts or legs
600ml (1 pint) chicken stock
  or water
2 sprigs of tarragon
75ml (2 1/2 fl oz) mayonnaise
  (see recipe on page 82, but
  omit the garlic and herbs)
75ml (2 1/2 fl oz) natural yoghurt
2 tbsp chopped fresh tarragon
1 tbsp lemon juice
1 tsp Dijon mustard
75g (3oz) celery, very finely
  chopped (peel the tough
  outer parts off the stalks
  first)
4 spring onions, trimmed
  and very finely chopped
Salt and freshly ground black
  pepper

A proper afternoon tea with the girls is the perfect opportunity to take the time to make dainty, old-fashioned finger sandwiches. You can experiment with fillings and breads, and even cut them into different shapes with cookie cutters. You can serve them as open or closed sandwiches, or toast the bread if you wish. Here are some of my favourite fillings. Serve them cut very small on pretty cake stands or serving plates.

Scrambled eggs and chives

Break the eggs into a bowl, add the milk and some salt and pepper and whisk for about 10 seconds. Put the butter into a cold saucepan, add the egg mixture and stir continuously with a wooden spoon over a low heat until the mixture looks scrambled, but still soft and creamy. Allow to cool and then stir in the chives.

Goat's cheese and sundried tomatoes

Place the sundried tomatoes in a bowl, add the goat's cheese and herbs and stir to mix. Add a tablespoon of olive oil if it's too stiff. As an alternative, substitute caramelised onions for the sundried tomatoes. For a little crunchy extra, scatter crushed walnuts on top.

Tarragon chicken

Place the chicken breasts or legs in a medium-sized saucepan and just cover with the stock or water (sometimes I add a splash of white wine too). Add the tarragon sprigs and simmer for 10–12 minutes (or 20 minutes for legs) until the meat is cooked (cut it in half to make sure). Take off the heat and allow the chicken to cool in the liquid if you have time (otherwise take out the chicken as it will cool faster out of the stock, but will retain more moisture and flavour if it cools in the stock). Once cool, remove the chicken from the stock and chop into 1cm (1/2in) dice. In a bowl, mix together the mayonnaise, yoghurt, chopped tarragon, lemon juice and mustard and then add the chicken, celery and spring onions. Mix well and season to taste.

Prawn and basil pâté

Melt the butter in a sauté pan or frying pan on a medium heat. Add the onion, garlic and chilli sauce and toss in the pan for 3–4 minutes until the onions are cooked through. Add the prawns and toss in the pan for 1–2 minutes until cooked. Transfer to a food processor and whiz until the prawns are a bit rough in texture. Leave to cool, then add the cream cheese and pulse for a second or two until mixed. Turn out into a bowl and fold in the lime or lemon juice and chopped basil. Season to taste.

Smoked chicken and avocado

In a small bowl, mix together the smoked chicken, avocado and mayonnaise, adding the chopped parsley, if using. Season to taste.

Smoked salmon and cucumber

On each slice of bread, lay a piece of smoked salmon and squeeze over some lemon juice. Cover with cucumber slices, a good grinding of black pepper and scatter over the herbs of your choice.

Pear and blue cheese

On each slice of bread (I like this best on walnut bread), lay a slice of Stilton. Add a couple of slices of pear and, if feeling especially greedy, add a slice of Parma ham.

PRAWN AND BASIL PÂTÉ
25g (1oz) butter
½ small onion, peeled and chopped
2 cloves of garlic, peeled and crushed or grated
200g (7oz) raw peeled prawns
1 tsp sweet chilli sauce
2 tbsp cream cheese
1–2 tbsp lime or lemon juice
1 tbsp chopped fresh basil
Salt and freshly ground black pepper

SMOKED CHICKEN AND AVOCADO
1–2 hot smoked (cooked) chicken breasts, chopped
1 avocado, peeled, stoned and chopped
3 tbsp mayonnaise (see recipe on page 82, but omit the garlic and herbs)
1 tbsp chopped parsley (optional)
Salt and freshly ground black pepper

SMOKED SALMON AND CUCUMBER
1 slice of salmon per sandwich
1 lemon, cut into quarters
Thin slices of cucumber
Freshly ground black pepper
2 tbsp chopped fennel, dill or chives

PEAR AND BLUE CHEESE
Thin slice of blue per sandwich
A couple of slices of pear per sandwich
Parma ham (optional extra)

Champagne Cocktails

SERVES 2
VEGETARIAN
2 sugar cubes
4 dashes of Angostura bitters
30ml (1fl oz) brandy
Chilled dry champagne,
    to top up

What could be more decadent than to enjoy a classic champagne cocktail with your afternoon tea?

1 Place a sugar cube in each champagne flute and moisten with the Angostura bitters.
2 Add the brandy, stir and then gently fill up to the top with the chilled champagne. Serve.

Variation

For something a little lighter and more fruity, pour equal quantities of champagne and peach and raspberry juice (see page 102) into your favourite flutes. For a classic Bellini cocktail, omit the raspberries and just use the peach juice.

Pleasure Without the Guilt

There is often nothing better than hearty comfort food but sometimes we all need a little reprieve from heavy dishes, particularly after the holidays. It's important to have a few recipes up your sleeve that feature wonderful, lively ingredients that push all the right pleasure buttons for those times when you want something just a little bit lighter. My feeling is that food should always be enjoyable and that you should never feel deprived. After all, where's the fun in a plain plate of iceberg lettuce?

Zac's Aztec Soup

This is Isaac's version of the classic Aztec soup. It's so wonderfully fresh and light, yet filling and nutritious. I never tire of eating this.

SERVES 4–6

3 tbsp olive oil

2 onions, peeled and chopped

Salt and freshly ground
   black pepper

4 large cloves of garlic, peeled
   and chopped or grated

1 tsp chopped and seeded
   red chilli

1 litre (1¾ pints) light
   chicken stock

1 large chicken breast, diced
   into 1cm (½in) pieces

Juice of ½ a lime

FOR THE SALSA

3 spring onions, trimmed
   and finely sliced

1 ripe avocado, peeled,
   stoned and diced into
   5mm (¼in) pieces

150g (5oz) tomatoes (or cherry
   tomatoes), diced

Juice of ½ lime

2 tbsp chopped coriander

Salt and freshly ground
   black pepper

1 Heat the olive oil in a large saucepan over a medium heat and add the chopped onion; season with salt and pepper. Cover and sweat for 10 minutes or until the onion is soft. Add the garlic and chilli and cook for 2 minutes. Add the stock and bring up to the boil, reduce to a simmer, add in the chicken and gently cook for 2–3 minutes until the meat is cooked. Turn off the heat, then add the lime juice.
2 Make the salsa by mixing all the ingredients together, season with salt and pepper.
3 To serve, ladle the hot soup into warm bowls and drop a large tablespoon of the salsa into each bowl.

Salad with Beetroot, Goat's Cheese and Toasted Hazelnuts

There is just enough goat's cheese in this salad to make it seem like a sneaky treat!

· ——————————— · ✿ · ——————————— ·

1 To make the dressing, mix together the vinegar and the olive oil, and season to taste.

2 Place the chopped beetroot and hazelnuts in a bowl, drizzle with three-quarters of the dressing, season and toss.

3 Place the salad leaves on one big serving plate or divide between individual plates and drizzle with the remaining dressing. Scatter the leaves with the beetroot and the hazelnuts, then break the goat's cheese into small pieces and arrange over the salad.

SERVES 4
VEGETARIAN
4 small beetroot (about 150g/5oz in total), cooked, peeled and cut into 1cm (1/2in) dice
40g (1³/₄oz) hazelnuts, toasted and roughly chopped
4 handfuls of salad leaves
150g (5oz) soft goat's cheese

FOR THE DRESSING
2 tsp balsamic vinegar
1 tbsp olive oil
Sea salt and freshly ground black pepper

Squid, Cucumber and Tomato Salad with a Black Olive and Basil Vinaigrette

SERVES 4

4 small or 2 large ripe
    tomatoes, cut into wedges
1/2 small cucumber, cut into
    wedges
1 generous tbsp sliced or
    torn fresh basil
1 generous tbsp finely
    chopped black olives
Sea salt and freshly ground
    black pepper
450g (1lb) squid, cleaned
    out and cut into rings or
    strips 5mm (1/4in) thick
2 tbsp olive oil
4 handfuls of rocket

FOR THE DRESSING

60ml (2fl oz) olive oil
30ml (1fl oz) balsamic vinegar
1 small clove of garlic, peeled
    and crushed or grated
Salt, freshly ground black
    pepper and a pinch of sugar

This is a wonderfully fresh salad with a tangy dressing, just perfect for an alfresco lunch on a warm and sunny summer's day.

· ❧ ·

1 To make the dressing, mix the olive oil, balsamic vinegar and garlic in a jar or small bowl. Season with salt, pepper and sugar.
2 For the salad, place the tomatoes, cucumber, basil and olives in a bowl and season.
3 Place a medium-sized frying pan on the heat and allow to get very hot. Place the squid in a bowl, add the oil and season with salt and pepper. Toss the squid in the hot pan and cook for 1–2 minutes only until deep golden in colour at the edges. Don't cook for too long or it will become rubbery.
4 Toss the squid with the cucumber and tomatoes. Drizzle with the dressing and season to taste. Divide the rocket leaves between four plates and top with the squid.

Baked Fish with Tomato, Cucumber and Ginger Salsa

SERVES 4

FOR THE SALSA

6 tbsp rice vinegar or white
   wine vinegar
2 tbsp fish sauce (nam pla)
50g (2oz) sugar
400g (14oz) tomatoes, diced
   into 1cm (1/2in) pieces
1 cucumber, deseeded and
   diced into 1cm (1/2in) pieces
1 small red onion, peeled
   and finely diced
1 spring onion, trimmed
   and finely diced
1/2–1 red chilli, deseeded
   and finely diced
Juice of 1/2 lime
2 tbsp chopped fresh
   coriander
1 tsp finely grated ginger

FOR THE FISH

4 portions (150g–175g/5–6oz
   each) fish, such as salmon,
   tuna, mackerel, mullet or
   sea bass, off the bone but
   leave the skin on if you
   wish (descale if it's salmon,
   mullet or bass)
Salt and freshly ground black
   pepper

This is a lovely light main course and looks so impressive served in the parchment paper it's cooked in. You'll hardly feel guilty after eating this!

1 Preheat the oven to 180°C (350°F), Gas mark 4.

2 Make the salsa first. Boil the vinegar, fish sauce and sugar (stir to dissolve the sugar) for 5 minutes until it thickens slightly. Place in a large mixing bowl and leave to cool. Then add the tomatoes, cucumber, onion, chilli, lime juice, coriander and ginger, toss and add more lime juice or ginger if necessary.

3 Place each fish on a large piece of oiled parchment paper or tin foil and season with salt and pepper. Then roll up the edges of the paper or foil to prevent the juices from burning in the dish. Cook in the oven for 12–18 minutes or until the fish is cooked through to the centre. Place the parcels on warmed serving plates and serve with the salsa. It is also good served at room temperature.

Chicken and Puy Lentil Salad with Coriander

SERVES 4

2 large or 4 small chicken
    breasts, skinned
1 tbsp whole coriander seeds,
    toasted and ground
2 large cloves of garlic, peeled
    and crushed or grated
Salt and freshly ground
    black pepper
Juice of 1 lemon
5 tbsp olive oil
225g (8oz) puy lentils
3 tbsp chopped fresh coriander
    (stalks and leaves)
100g (4oz) mixed salad
    leaves, such as rocket,
    baby beetroot, baby
    spinach and frisée
100g (4oz) feta cheese,
    crumbled
Balsamic vinegar

This is a delicious and light, yet surprisingly substantial salad so there's little chance you'll be left feeling hungry.

1 Using a sharp knife, make a few long shallow incisions on both sides of the chicken breasts. Place in a bowl. Add the ground coriander, garlic, a pinch of black pepper, 2 tablespoons of lemon juice and 2 tablespoons of the olive oil. Mix into the chicken, making sure all the meat is evenly coated in the marinade. Allow to sit for about 30 minutes (or 1 hour if you have the time).

2 Preheat the oven to 230°C (450°F), Gas mark 8.

3 When the oven is good and hot, spread the chicken out on a baking tray and cook it for 15–30 minutes, depending on the size of the chicken breasts. To ensure the chicken is cooked through, cut into the breast with a knife. Once cooked, take the chicken out of the oven and allow it to rest for a couple of minutes.

4 Meanwhile, place the lentils in a saucepan, cover with water and boil for about 20 minutes, until cooked through. When cooked, drain the lentils then dress them with the remaining olive oil, lemon juice and chopped coriander, and season with salt and pepper.

5 To assemble the salad, slice the chicken thinly and toss with the lentils (they can be still warm) and the mixed salad leaves. Place on plates or in a large bowl and sprinkle with the crumbled feta and a small drizzle of balsamic vinegar.

Asian Chicken Salad

This salad pushes all the right flavour buttons without being heavy or stodgy. The spicy flavour makes it a very satisfying meal.

—————————————— · ✿ · ——————————————

1 Mix together the garlic, ginger, chilli, lemon juice, soy sauce, fish sauce and sugar in a small bowl. Cut the chicken into pieces the size of a finger.

2 Heat a frying pan or wok until hot and smokey. Add the oil, then the chicken. Toss in the pan for a few minutes until just cooked, then add in the dressing and let it boil for a minute.

3 Take off the heat and empty into a large mixing bowl. Add the salad leaves and nearly all the peanuts and toss quickly. Tip onto one large or four individual plates, scatter with the remaining peanuts and serve immediately.

SERVES 4 AS A LIGHT LUNCH

2 cloves of garlic, peeled and chopped
2 tsp finely chopped ginger
1–2 tsp chopped red chilli
Juice of 1/2 lemon
1 tbsp soy sauce
1 tbsp fish sauce (nam pla)
1 level tbsp sugar
500g (1lb 2oz) chicken breasts, skinned
2 tbsp sunflower oil or sesame oil
2 tbsp chopped peanuts
4 handfuls of mixed salad leaves

Chicken with Lemon and Honey

This is one of the simplest and most delicious ways to cook chicken. Although the recipe does include a small amount of honey, it does not call for any added oil so is definitely high on pleasure and low on guilt.

1 Preheat the oven to 180°C (350°F), Gas mark 4.

2 Place the chicken pieces in a large baking dish, skin side up (they can be skinned if you prefer but I usually leave the skin on). In a small bowl mix the juice of the lemons with the honey, then pour this over the chicken pieces. Place the empty lemon halves in the dish too for extra flavour. Season with sea salt and pepper and place the sprigs of rosemary or thyme between the chicken pieces.

3 Cook in the oven for 40 minutes or until the chicken is cooked and the skin is golden. Remove from the oven and discard the lemon halves. Pour the juices from the dish into a saucepan and boil, uncovered, for about 5 minutes until the juices have thickened slightly. Taste and add more salt and pepper if necessary. Serve the chicken and sauce with a salad or rice.

SERVES 4

1 chicken, cut into pieces, or 8 chicken pieces (breasts, legs or thighs)
2 lemons
2 tbsp honey
Sea salt and freshly ground black pepper
2 sprigs of fresh rosemary or 6 sprigs of fresh thyme

Korean Beef with Avocado Rice

SERVES 4

400g (14oz) beef sirloin,
   cut into 2cm (¾in) dice
6 cloves of garlic, peeled
   and crushed
3 tbsp soy sauce
3 tbsp sesame seed oil
2 tbsp rice wine vinegar
2 tbsp soft light brown sugar
1 tbsp fish sauce (nam pla)
10 spring onions, dark green
   bits discarded
Salt
200g (7oz) long grain rice,
   like basmati
2 tbsp olive oil
2 avocados
Juice of ½ lime

TO SERVE

4 wedges of lime
A few sprigs of fresh
   coriander (optional)

Isaac makes this delicious Korean-inspired beef dish; it's great for a dinner party, and of course the beef and spring onion satays can be cooked on the barbecue too. The avocado in the rice is an unusual addition, but one that works very well. Of course, this recipe isn't totally guilt free but it is relatively nutritious and so delicious that it's worth every bite.

1 Place 8 satay sticks in a saucepan of boiling water and boil for 2 minutes, which will stop them from charring or, even worse, going up in flames, when cooking the beef in step 5. Drain and set the satay sticks aside.

2 Prepare the beef by mixing it with the crushed garlic, soy sauce, sesame seed oil, rice wine vinegar, brown sugar and fish sauce. Place in a plastic bag or a bowl and add the beef. Stir to mix, cover and leave to marinate in the fridge for 1–2 hours, if possible.

3 Cut the spring onions into 2cm (¾in) lengths. Remove the beef from the marinade, but reserve the marinade for later. Thread the beef and the spring onion pieces alternately on the satay sticks, with about 4 pieces of each on each stick.

4 Bring a saucepan of water up to the boil, add a good pinch of salt and the rice. Boil for 7–8 minutes, until cooked. Drain, then stir in the olive oil and cover with a saucepan lid or a plate and keep warm until you are ready to serve.

5 Heat up a grill pan or large frying pan until very hot. Add the beef and spring onion satay sticks, placed in a single layer on the very hot pan. Cook on each side for about 2–3 minutes until cooked to your liking. Pour the reserved marinade into the pan and allow it to bubble and boil – it will reduce down and intensify in flavour.

6 While the beef is cooking, peel the avocados and chop the flesh into 1cm (½in) dice. Drizzle with the lime juice and mix. When you are ready to serve, mix the avocados with the rice and season with salt to taste. Serve the avocado rice with the beef skewers on warm plates or in bowls with a wedge of lime on the side. If you wish, you can decorate with coriander leaves.

Yoghurt, Cardamom and Orange Panna Cotta

For this recipe I have replaced cream with yoghurt, so it is not a true panna cotta. However, the yoghurt creates a light and refreshing dessert, and the flavours of the cardamom, orange and honey make it wonderfully fragrant and exotic. Serve in espresso cups or little glasses on its own, or with some strawberries or raspberries. I adore this after a spicy curry.

SERVES 4–6
1 leaf of gelatine
200ml (7fl oz) milk
2 generous tbsp honey
Scant 1/2 tsp ground
  cardamom seeds
175ml (6fl oz) natural yoghurt
1 tsp finely grated orange zest

1 Place the gelatine in a bowl of cold water and leave to soak for 5 minutes until soft.

2 Place the milk, honey and ground cardamom seeds in a saucepan and slowly bring up to the boil. Drop in the softened gelatine and stir to dissolve and set aside for about 10 minutes or until it has reached room temperature.

3 Place the yoghurt and orange zest in another bowl and add the milk, whisking to mix it. Pour the mixture into little glasses or cups and place in the fridge for 2 hours until set. Serve chilled straight from the fridge.

Fresh Fruit Sorbets

EACH SERVES 4
VEGETARIAN

PEAR SORBET
3 small or 2 medium pears,
  peeled, cored and quartered
Juice of 2 large or 3 small
  lemons
75g (3oz) caster sugar
150ml (¼ pint) water

MELON AND LIME SORBET
½ ripe melon, such as Ogen
  or Charentais (about
  400g/14oz)
Juice of 1 large or 2 small limes
30ml (1fl oz) stock syrup (see
  handy tip)

**RASPBERRY AND
BLUEBERRY SORBET**
125g (4½oz) raspberries
  (can be frozen)
125g (4½oz) blueberries
  (can be frozen)
Juice of 1 large lemon
60ml (2fl oz) stock syrup
  (see handy tip)

If you fancy a frozen dessert but don't want the heaviness of ice cream, sorbets are just the ticket. These ones are real crowd-pleasers and are perfect as an afternoon treat on a hot summer's day.

Pear sorbet
Place the pears in a small saucepan with the juice of half a lemon and the sugar and water. Cook on a medium heat until the pears are just soft, about 10 minutes. Remove the pears and boil the cooking liquid until it's slightly thick and syrupy. Allow to cool then liquidise it with the pears and the rest of the lemon juice and sieve. Taste and adjust juice if necessary. Then follow the freezing method below.

Melon and lime sorbet
Liquidise all the ingredients in a food processor and push through a sieve to strain. Freeze as below.

Raspberry and blueberry sorbet
Liquidise all the ingredients in a food processor and push through a sieve to strain. Freeze as below.

To freeze
Pop the liquid sorbet into a medium-sized bowl, cover and place in the freezer. After about 2 hours, remove the bowl and whisk the sorbet to break up the ice crystals. Repeat 2 hours later, adding one slightly whisked egg white. If you have a sorbetière, use this instead as it is much simpler. Follow the manufacturer's instructions.

Rachel's handy tip

Stock syrup is a useful mixture to have at hand for such things as cocktails and poaching fruit, as well as for making sorbet. Store it in a jar or bottle with a lid in a cool place and it keeps indefinitely. To make 150ml (¼ pint), place 200g (7oz) caster sugar and 200ml (7fl oz) water in a saucepan and bring slowly to the boil, stirring to dissolve the sugar. Then boil for 2 minutes and leave to cool.

Food for Romance

Beautiful and delicious food really can be the way to someone's heart. Whether you're planning your first dinner together or your fiftieth anniversary, a special romantic meal should be a memorable experience. It doesn't have to be lavish – sometimes a little loving treat can say more than words. These are some of my favourite ways to say 'I love you', and for obvious reasons all recipes are for two!

Heart-shaped Toast with Eggs, Asparagus and Truffle Hollandaise Sauce

SERVES 2
VEGETARIAN

FOR THE TRUFFLE HOLLANDAISE SAUCE AND ASPARAGUS
1 large egg yolk
50g (2oz) butter, cut into cubes
1 tsp white truffle oil
6 large or 10 small asparagus stalks
Salt
Knob of butter

FOR THE TOAST
2 thick slices of good white bread, each slice 2cm (½in) thick
15g (½oz) butter,
2 eggs

I know there is a bit of work involved in making this, but this is the ultimate romantic breakfast in bed. The divine truffle hollandaise sauce is just a simple variation on a basic hollandaise but takes it to another dimension altogether. It works well with fish, too. If you don't have truffle oil, just serve it with plain hollandaise. Don't worry – you'll still get a kiss!

1 To make the hollandaise sauce, place the egg yolk in a heatproof bowl. Heat the butter in a saucepan until it is foaming, and then pour gradually onto the egg yolk, whisking all the time. Add the truffle oil and then pour into a heatproof measuring jug. Half-fill a saucepan with hot water from the kettle and place the jug of hollandaise in the saucepan to keep warm; it will sit quite happily like this for a couple of hours. When the water cools, just put the saucepan on a gentle heat but do not let the water boil too long or the sauce will scramble.

2 Remove the tough woody ends from the asparagus stalks by simply snapping them off. Discard. Place a large saucepan on the heat with about 3cm (1¼in) of water in it. Add a good pinch of salt and cook the asparagus, uncovered, for 3–6 minutes, until just soft. Drain and return to the saucepan. Add a small knob of butter and toss to coat the asparagus. Keep warm.

3 Using a heart-shaped cutter or knife, cut out heart shapes from the slices of bread). Heat a medium-sized frying pan on a medium heat and preheat a grill to hot. Place the butter in the pan and, once melted, add the slices of bread. Break each egg into each cut-out heart shape and cook on the heat until the bread is golden underneath and the egg white is looking opaque.

4 Take it off the heat and place under the grill and cook until the bread is slightly toasted and the eggs are cooked. Transfer to two warmed plates, drizzle with the truffle hollandaise sauce and arrange the asparagus around the toast on the plate. Serve and watch him or her swoon!

Oysters

Of course, oysters are the oldest trick in the book when it comes to culinary seduction! Or so they say. Whether or not this is scientifically accurate is still open to debate, so you may as well experiment to see if it's true for you. Here are two delicious ways to do just that.

· ♡ ·

First things first: how to open an oyster

It is best to use an oyster knife, which is designed for the purpose and will make your life much easier (and safer). If you don't have an oyster knife, you can use a thin chisel, but do not attempt to open oysters with any knife that has a bendy blade. Oysters are at their best when there is an 'r' in the month (in other words, during the colder months) when they are not spawning. They are much creamier in texture during these months.

1 Fold a tea towel lengthwise and wrap it around your hand once or twice to protect yourself from the knife in case of slippage. Place the oyster on the remaining edge of the towel, with the flatter side of the oyster facing up. You will see a slight crevice where the shells meet at the narrow end.

2 Take your oyster knife (or thin clean chisel) and insert the blade into the crevice while holding the opposite end steady with your wrapped hand. Press and turn the knife, levering upwards. Once the shell pops open, insert a clean knife just under the top shell to cut the oyster away – it will suddenly free.

3 Cut the membrane where the oyster is attached to the shell and remove the oyster altogether or replace it on the shell, discarding any bits of broken shell. Serve as soon as possible or at least within 24 hours. Store refrigerated in a sealed container until serving.

OYSTERS WITH BLOODY
MARY SHOTS
MAKES 4 SHOTS
4 fresh raw oysters, opened
1/2 small stalk of celery, very
    finely chopped
1/2 tsp Worcestershire sauce
Few drops Tabasco sauce
Small pinch of celery salt
    or sea salt
Small pinch of sugar
2 tsp freshly squeezed lemon
    juice
Pinch of grated horseradish
    (optional)
200ml (7fl oz) tomato juice
75ml (2 1/2fl oz) vodka
2 tsp sweet sherry (or dry
    sherry with an extra pinch
    of sugar)

OYSTERS WITH CUCUMBER
AND GINGER SALSA
SERVES 2
2 tbsp rice vinegar (or white
    wine vinegar)
1 tbsp fish sauce (nam pla)
1 generous tbsp caster sugar
1/4 large cucumber, cut in
    half lengthways, seeds
    discarded and very finely
    diced
1 tbsp very finely chopped
    red onion
1 tbsp finely chopped spring
    onion
1 level tsp finely grated ginger
1/4–1/2 red chilli, deseeded and
    finely chopped
A squeeze of lime juice
24 fresh oysters, opened and
    on the half-shell (top shell
    discarded)

Oysters with Bloody Mary Shots

This is such a great combination and a fun, novel way to serve oysters.

1 Place one raw oyster in each shot glass and divide the chopped celery between the glasses too.
2 For the Bloody Mary, mix together all the remaining ingredients, seasoning to taste. Shake with ice in a cocktail shaker or mix the Bloody Mary in a jug with ice to chill it, then strain (to remove the ice) and pour into the glasses on top of the oysters and serve.

Oysters with Cucumber and Ginger Salsa

This salsa recipe is wonderfully light and zingy and makes enough for about two-dozen oysters, but you can reduce or multiply the quantities accordingly.

1 To make the salsa, place the vinegar, fish sauce and sugar in a small saucepan and bring to the boil, stirring to dissolve the sugar. Remove the spoon and boil for 1–2 minutes until the syrup has thickened slightly. Pour into a mixing bowl and leave to cool.
2 When the salsa is cool add the cucumber, red and spring onions, ginger, chilli and about 1 tablespoon of lime juice. Mix with the syrup and taste; it may need more lime juice or ginger. Store in the fridge for up to a few hours until you need it.
3 When you are ready to serve, place the oysters sitting in their shells on a plate and spoon a small teaspoonful of the salsa over each oyster and serve.

Crab and Prawn Coconut Soup

As with lobster, crab and prawns are also quintessential foods for romance and indulgence. This soup is delightfully rich and flavoursome but as it contains coconut milk rather than cream it will not leave you feeling sluggish!

———— · ♡ · ————

1 In a large saucepan on a medium heat, heat the oil, then add the garlic, ginger, lemon grass and crab meat. Toss on the heat for a few minutes until light golden. Add the stock, coconut milk and fish sauce. Bring to the boil, reduce to a simmer and add the prawns. 2 Cook for 1–2 minutes (simmering all the time) until the prawns are cooked. Then add the spring onions, lemon juice, chilli and coriander, season to taste and serve.

SERVES 2

2 tbsp sunflower oil
2 small cloves of garlic, peeled and sliced
1/2 tsp grated ginger
1 tsp lemon grass, finely chopped
200g (7oz) crab meat
500ml (18fl oz) fish or light chicken stock
1 x 165g tin coconut milk
1 tbsp fish sauce (nam pla)
50g (2oz) raw prawns, peeled
2 spring onions, trimmed and finely sliced
Juice of 1/2 lemon
1/4 red chilli, deseeded and finely chopped
1 tbsp chopped fresh coriander (leaves and stalks)
Salt and freshly ground black pepper

Pan-fried Scallops with Truffle Beurre Blanc

SERVES 2

FOR THE BEURRE BLANC
2 tbsp white wine
2 tbsp white wine vinegar
2 tsp finely chopped shallot
1 tbsp single cream
100g (4oz) butter, diced
A wedge of lemon
Salt and freshly ground
    black pepper
1 tsp truffle oil (depending
    how strong the oil is)

FOR THE SCALLOPS
7 scallops
Sunflower or olive oil
    (optional)

TO SERVE
A few fennel, chervil or
flat parsley leaves

Your lover (or intended lover!) will think you are a genius if you cook this recipe. Scallops are one of the easiest things to cook and, of course, very sensual to eat.

· ———————————— · ♡ · ———————————— ·

1 To make the beurre blanc, place the wine, vinegar and shallot in a medium-sized saucepan, boil and reduce the liquid until there is only about 1 tablespoon left in the pan. Add the cream and boil again for about 10 seconds until the cream thickens slightly. Remove from the heat and allow to cool for 1 minute. When you can hold your hands on the sides of the pan without it being too hot, you can start to whisk in the butter, over a very low heat, two pieces at a time. If the pan gets too warm, take it off the heat for a second (otherwise the sauce can curdle). When all the butter is added, add a squeeze of lemon juice and, if you used unsalted butter, you will also need a pinch of salt.

2 Keep the sauce warm by placing it in a heatproof jug. Half-fill a saucepan with hot water from the kettle and place the jug of sauce in the saucepan to keep warm; it will sit quite happily like this for a couple of hours. When the water cools, just put the saucepan on a gentle heat but do not let the water boil too long or the sauce will scramble. As it sits, it may thicken slightly, in which case thin out with a few drops of warm water just before serving.

3 Next, prepare the scallops. If they still have the membrane around them, pull this off and discard. Slice the round scallop in half horizontally and keep the corals whole. Wash and dry the scallops and corals. Season with salt and pepper and preheat a medium-sized frying pan. If you are using a non-stick pan, you will not need any oil when cooking the scallops; otherwise, wipe the pan with a tiny bit of olive oil. Allow the pan to get hot on a medium heat. Cook the scallops and corals on each side for a minute or so until they are golden brown. Add the truffle oil to the beurre blanc.

4 Place seven halves and one or two corals on each plate and drizzle with the truffle beurre blanc. Decorate with a few fennel, chervil or flat parsley leaves and serve.

Fish Cakes with Lemon and Pine Nuts

These are such lovely little fish cakes. The savoury pink sauce looks quite delightful and tastes delicious!

— · ♡ · —

1 First make the sauce. Whiz or liquidise the tomatoes and garlic, strain into a small bowl and stir in the yoghurt and mint, season to taste with a pinch of salt, pepper and sugar. Set aside while you make the fish cakes.

2 Place a wide frying or sauté pan on the heat, allow to get slightly hot, then add half the oil, fish and ground coriander. Toss in the pan for 2 minutes until the fish is just opaque. In a bowl, mix the remaining ingredients, except the egg, and add the cooked fish. Add enough beaten egg to bring it together to a softish mixture (if the egg is very large you may not need it all). Season to taste, then shape it into 4 fish cakes in your hands.

3 For the coriander dressing, mix together the olive oil, lemon juice and coriander and season to taste, adding more lemon juice if necessary.

4 To cook the fish cakes, place a frying pan on a medium heat, heat the remaining oil and put in the fish cakes. Turn down the heat slightly and cook gently for 3–4 minutes on each side until golden brown on both sides. Place the fish cakes on two warmed plates and serve with the tomato, yoghurt and mint sauce and the watercress salad drizzled with just enough dressing to make the leaves glisten.

Rachel's handy tip ♡

To toast the pine nuts (or any other kind of nut), toss them in a dry pan for 2–3 minutes until golden over a high heat.

SERVES 2

FOR THE TOMATO, YOGHURT AND MINT SAUCE
1 large or 2 small ripe
  tomatoes, chopped
1 clove of garlic, peeled
  and crushed
2 tbsp natural yoghurt
2 tsp chopped mint
Salt, freshly ground black
  pepper and a pinch of sugar

FOR THE FISH CAKES
4 tbsp peanut or sunflower oil
200g (7oz) skinless haddock,
  hake, salmon or cod, cut
  into 1cm (1/2in) dice
2 tsp ground coriander seeds
2 tbsp chopped fresh
  coriander or dill
25g (1oz) Parmesan cheese,
  finely grated
75g (3oz) white breadcrumbs
  (can be frozen)
Finely grated zest and juice
  of 1/2 lemon
50g (2oz) toasted pine nuts
1 large egg, whisked

FOR THE WATERCRESS SALAD
WITH CORIANDER DRESSING
2 tbsp olive oil
2–3 tsp lemon juice
1 tbsp chopped coriander
A few large handfuls of
  watercress leaves, thicker
  stalks removed

Arabian Spiced Rack of Lamb with Couscous

SERVES 2

FOR THE HARISSA PASTE
MAKES ABOUT 150ML
(¼ PINT)
25g (1oz) dried large red chillies
2 tbsp coriander seeds
1 generous tbsp cumin seeds
2 cloves of garlic, peeled
1 tsp salt
60ml (2fl oz) olive oil
¼ tsp ground paprika

FOR THE RACK OF LAMB
1 prepared rack of lamb
    (2–3 cutlets per person
    depending on their size
    and your appetite!)
Salt and freshly ground
    black pepper

FOR THE COUSCOUS
100g (4oz) couscous
2 tbsp olive oil
150ml (¼ pint) light chicken
    or vegetable stock
1 tbsp chopped fresh parsley
2 tbsp chopped fresh mint
½ red onion, peeled and
    finely chopped
50g (2oz) flaked almonds,
    toasted

TO SERVE
Greek yoghurt (optional)

A small rack of lamb is absolutely perfect for serving two people, allowing three or four cutlets per person. This recipe has wonderful warm and spicy Moroccan flavours, perfect for a romantic, cosy dinner for two. Spices also always raise the endorphin levels, so you feel energised! This recipe contains harissa, a versatile and very hot North African paste that can be added to dishes or served separately in a bowl on the table. It is available to buy in many shops but for a delicious fresh flavour you can make your own. It will keep in the fridge in a covered jar for a few weeks. If you are concerned about the heat of the paste, use milder chillis.

1 To make the harissa paste, split the chillies in half lengthways, remove and discard the seeds and soften the chillies in boiling water for 5 minutes. Meanwhile, dry-fry the coriander and cumin seeds in a frying pan on a medium to high heat for about 1 minute, tossing regularly, until the spices just begin to smoke and toast. Then grind in a spice grinder or use a mortar and pestle.
2 Place the garlic, salt, ground spices and the drained red chillies in a food processor and whiz to a paste, slowly adding the olive oil until well combined. Set aside.
3 Preheat the oven to 220°C (425°F), Gas mark 7.
4 Next, prepare the rack of lamb. Score the fat lightly in a criss-cross pattern, but without cutting through to the meat. Place the lamb in a roasting tray, spread a generous tablespoon of the harissa paste over the fat and press it down onto the fat with your hands or a spoon. Roast for 20 minutes for rare to medium, 25 minutes for well done for a small rack or 30–32 minutes for a larger rack. After 10 minutes, cover the rack with a sheet of tin foil to prevent the harissa paste from burning.
5 Meanwhile, prepare the couscous. Put it into a bowl, rub in the olive oil so that the grains are coated, and pour over the hot stock. Stir and then put a plate or saucepan lid on top and leave to stand for 5 minutes, until the couscous has absorbed all the stock. Add

the parsley, mint, onion and most of the toasted flaked almonds, stir well and season.

6 Once the lamb is cooked, turn off the oven and leave the meat to rest for 5–10 minutes. Carve it by cutting through the meat between the bones to give each person 2–3 cutlets (depending on the cutlet size). Spoon the couscous on to warmed plates and arrange the lamb cutlets on top. Scatter with the remaining toasted flaked almonds, and serve with a spoonful of Greek yogurt, if you wish.

Love Potions

EACH SERVES 2

VEGETARIAN

**PINK POMEGRANATE
COCKTAIL**

75ml (2½fl oz) lime juice

2 tbsp extra caster sugar or
coloured decorating sugar
on a saucer to dip in

Juice of 1 pomegranate or
60ml (2fl oz) pomegranate
juice from a carton

60ml (2fl oz) stock syrup
(see page 162)

75ml (2½fl oz) vodka or
Bacardi

About 1 cup of ice

**RHUBARB AND VODKA
COCKTAIL**

1 stalk rhubarb, finely sliced

50g (2oz) caster sugar

60ml (2fl oz) water

100ml (3½fl oz) vodka
(or white rum)

30–60ml (1–2fl oz) lime juice

Juice of 1 large orange

About ½ cup of ice

These whimsical cocktails are fun and festive – perfect for a date at home with your loved one!

Pink Pomegranate Cocktail

1 Take two martini or champagne glasses, dip the rim of the glasses in the lime juice and then into the sugar. Set the glasses aside in the freezer or fridge.

2 Mix the pomegranate juice, syrup, vodka and lime juice in a cocktail shaker (or jug) with the ice, shake and then strain (leaving the ice behind) into the chilled glasses.

Rhubarb and Vodka Cocktail

1 Place four cocktail glasses in the freezer.

2 Place the rhubarb, sugar and water in a saucepan and bring to the boil, stirring to dissolve the sugar. Allow to boil for a few minutes until the rhubarb has broken down to a mush. Take off the heat and allow to cool. If you are concerned that the mixture looks too thick, strain it through a sieve before using.

3 When it's cool, add the vodka and lime and orange juices. Shake in a cocktail shaker or stir in a jug with the ice, then strain (leaving the ice behind) into the chilled glasses.

Rachel's handy tips

❀ If making the pink pomegranate cocktail with a fresh pomegranate, get the juice by cutting it in half and squeezing the halves into a sieve sitting over a bowl. Reserve a few of the pomegranate seeds and float them in each glass.

❀ If you are concerned that the cooked rhubarb looks too thick for rhubarb and vodka cocktail, strain it before using.

Light and Fluffy White Chocolate Mousse

This is the most divine dessert, especially for white-chocolate lovers. Serve on its own or with seasonal berries.

— · ♡ · —

1 Melt the chocolate in a bowl sitting over a saucepan of simmering water (also known as a bain marie). Set aside, leaving the chocolate to cool slightly. Whip the cream in a separate bowl until it is almost stiff and place in the fridge.

2 Place the gelatine in a small bowl of cold water for 3–4 minutes until it has softened. Drain off the water and then add 2 tablespoons of boiling water and stir to dissolve the gelatine.

3 Place the egg white in a medium-sized bowl with half the sugar, whisk until it's firm and then add the remaining sugar and continue whisking until the mixture is stiff.

4 Pour the dissolved gelatine into the melted chocolate and stir to mix, then fold in the whisked egg white mixture and, lastly, fold in the cool whipped cream. Pour into glasses or bowls, cover and place in the fridge for a couple of hours until just set.

SERVES 2

50g (2oz) white chocolate, chopped
75ml (2½fl oz) double cream
½ leaf of gelatine
1 large egg white
25g (1oz) caster sugar

Little Mocha Kisses

**MAKES ABOUT 25 KISSES
(LEFTOVERS WILL KEEP IN
A CONTAINER FOR 2–3 DAYS)
VEGETARIAN**

175g (6oz) self-raising flour
75g (3oz) caster sugar
75g (3oz) butter
2 tsp instant coffee powder
  or granules
1 tsp hot water
1 egg

FOR THE CHOCOLATE ICING
50g (2oz) butter, softened
100g (4oz) icing sugar
3 tsp cocoa powder

These tiny heart-shaped biscuits make a sweet and loving way to end a romantic meal. Serve them with a cup of coffee after dinner.

1 Preheat the oven to 180°C (350°F), Gas mark 4.

2 Place the flour, sugar and butter in a food processor and whiz until the mixture resembles breadcrumbs. In a cup or small bowl, mix the coffee with the hot water, then add the egg and whisk to break up. Add this into the food processor and process until the dough comes together. (If making this by hand, rub the butter into the flour and sugar in a bowl, then add the coffee, water and egg mixture and bring together to a dough.)

3 Dust the work surface with icing sugar and then roll out the dough until it is 5mm (1/4in) thick and, using a small, 4cm (11/2in) long heart-shaped cutter, cut out 50–60 heart shapes. Place them slightly spaced apart on two baking trays (no need to grease) and bake in the oven for 10–15 minutes or until golden brown and slightly firm at the edges. Remove from the oven and carefully lift off the tray with a metal slice while they are still very hot to prevent them sticking. Allow to cool on a wire rack.

4 To make the chocolate icing, in a bowl using a wooden spoon, or in the food processor again, mix the soft butter, icing sugar and cocoa powder until it comes together. Use the icing to sandwich the cookies together (see the photograph on page 184). If you dip a table knife into hot water as you work, it helps to spread the icing. Store in a box for two or three days.

Rachel's handy tip

If you find the dough is a bit soft before shaping, chill it in the deep freeze for 10 minutes before using.

For the Love of Chocolate

*The last time I wrote about chocolate
I received more mail than for any other
subject. I soon realised that chocolate is
almost an emotion in its own right! People
who love chocolate often say they can't
live without it. This single food inspires
such extraordinary passion that it seemed
essential to dedicate an entire chapter to
it. So, for all you chocoholics, this one is
for you!*

Chocolate Amaretti Cake

SERVES 8–12
VEGETARIAN

150g (5oz) good dark chocolate (at least 55% cocoa solids, 70% makes this even richer and more wonderful)
50g (2oz) Amaretti biscuits
100g (4oz) flaked slivered almonds
175g (7oz) caster sugar
Finely grated zest of 1 orange
100g (4oz) butter, cut into cubes
4 eggs, beaten
Cocoa powder or icing sugar, for dusting

I tasted a cake rather like this in Italy years ago, served with a small glass of Amaretti liqueur on the side – divine! It is very moist on the inside and has a lovely bite from the almonds and Amaretti biscuits. It can be made a day or two in advance but, in fact, will keep incredibly well for a week.

1 Preheat the oven to 180°C (350°F), Gas mark 4. Line the base of a 20cm (8in) diameter spring-form tin with greaseproof paper and butter the sides (I usually just wipe a butter wrapper around the tin).
2 Melt the chocolate in a bowl sitting over a saucepan of simmering water (also known as a bain marie).
3 Place the Amaretti biscuits, flaked almonds, sugar and orange zest in a food processor and whiz until the biscuits and almonds are almost finely ground (I like to leave them a bit gritty). Add the butter and the eggs and whiz until blended, then add the melted chocolate and briefly whiz again until blended.
4 Pour the mixture into the prepared tin and pop straight into the oven. Cook for 35 minutes until the cake is puffed up and slightly cracked around the edges. Remove from the oven and leave to sit for 15 minutes before carefully transferring to a plate. The top is quite crisp and cracks easily so I always dust it with lots of icing sugar or cocoa powder before serving to hide any imperfections!

Rachel's handy tip

If you don't have a food processor, you will need to use ground almonds instead of flaked and place the Amaretti biscuits in a plastic bag and grind up with a rolling pin. Beat in a large bowl in the same order as you do with the food processor.

Torta di Cappuccino

This is an absolutely delicious recipe and is a sure winner for any dinner party – so thank you to my friend Dervilla, for passing it on to me. It can be made a day in advance, which is always a bonus if you're feeding a crowd or planning a dinner party.

1 Preheat the oven to 180°C (350°F), Gas mark 4.

2 To make the base, crumble the biscuits into a medium-sized bowl, mix with the cream and butter and spread into a 23cm (9in) diameter, spring-form tin. Chill in the fridge while you make the topping.

3 For the topping and using an electric hand mixer, beat the mascarpone and sugar very well in a large bowl until soft and light. Break the eggs into a small bowl and whisk with a fork. Add to the cheese mixture, bit by bit, beating very well between each addition.

4 Melt the chocolate in a bowl sitting over a saucepan of simmering water (also known as a bain marie). Add the coffee liqueur and the espresso coffee to the melted chocolate and blend well. Then add to the cheese and egg mixture and also mix well.

5 Pour over the biscuit base and bake in the oven for 40–50 minutes until the centre is set; it shouldn't jiggle anymore! Leave to cool in the pan and then remove and serve lightly dusted with icing sugar or cocoa powder together with some lightly whipped cream.

SERVES 6
VEGETARIAN

FOR THE BASE
375g (13oz) dark chocolate wholewheat digestive biscuits
3 tbsp double cream
75g (3oz) butter, melted

FOR THE TOPPING
500g (1lb 2oz) mascarpone
140g (scant 5oz) caster sugar
3 eggs
100g (4oz) chocolate (at least 55% cocoa solids)
3 tbsp Kahlua or Tia Maria (coffee liqueur)
125ml (4fl oz) espresso or really strong coffee

TO SERVE
Icing sugar or cocoa powder
Lightly whipped cream

Stacked Chocolate Fudge Squares with White Chocolate and Raspberries

MAKES 25 SQUARES
VEGETARIAN

200g (7oz) dark chocolate,
   chopped
150g (5oz) butter
225g (8oz) caster sugar
3 eggs, beaten
150g (5oz) plain flour, sifted
1 tsp baking powder
225g (8oz) white chocolate,
   chopped
125g (4½oz) raspberries, plus
   a few extra to decorate

This recipe takes brownies to a new level. It is the ultimate sticky, gooey chocolate treat, and is incredibly easy to make. It looks really impressive without being complicated.

1 Preheat the oven to 180°C (350°F), Gas mark 4. Line a 20cm (8in) square deep baking tin with greaseproof paper and grease the base and sides.

2 In a large bowl sitting over simmering water (also known as a bain marie), melt the dark chocolate and butter. Stir in the sugar and then gradually add the eggs. Add the sifted flour and baking powder followed by 125g (4½oz) of the white chocolate and finally the raspberries.

3 Spread the mixture into the prepared tin and bake in the oven for 35–45 minutes or until just firm on top. Remove from the oven and let sit in the tin for another 30 minutes before cutting into squares and serving.

4 Melt the remaining white chocolate in a bowl sitting over simmering water. Stack the brownies on a plate or cake tray and when the chocolate is ready pour it over the top of the brownies. Decorate with a few fresh raspberries and watch your friends gasp with excitement.

Rachel's handy tip

These are deliciously moist so will keep for four or five days in an airtight container somewhere cool.

Chocolate Biscuit Cake

MAKES 16 SLICES
VEGETARIAN

150g (5oz) good-quality plain
    chocolate, chopped
150g (5oz) butter
2 large tbsp golden syrup
225g (8oz) semi-sweet
    biscuits, such as digestives,
    crushed (in a bowl with your
    hands, or in a plastic bag
    with a rolling pin)
25g (1oz) hazelnuts or
    almonds, toasted and
    chopped (optional)

This recipe requires no baking – it is simply left to set in the refrigerator after the ingredients are put together. The recipe was given to me by a friend, Ruth Douglas, and now it is one of my boys' favourites. It will keep in the fridge for up to two weeks, but with the boys around, it never lasts that long!

1 Melt the chocolate with the butter and golden syrup in a large bowl sitting over a saucepan of simmering water on a low heat.
2 Stir in the crushed biscuits and nuts (if using) until well blended. Spread into a 23cm (9in) diameter round cake tin or a 20cm (8in) square tin, lined with greaseproof or parchment paper.
3 Refrigerate for a couple of hours until well set, or pop into the freezer for 45 minutes. Cut into 16 pieces.

Variation
To turn this recipe into something a little different , add 25g (1oz) raisins that have been soaked in a couple of tablespoons of warmed brandy for a few minutes – perfect for serving with coffee at the end of a meal.

Chocolate Sticky Toffee Pudding

SERVES 6–8

VEGETARIAN

300ml (½ pint) boiling water
150g (5oz) chopped dates
100g (4oz) dark chocolate
100g (4oz) butter, softened
150g (5oz) soft light
    brown sugar or light
    muscovado sugar
3 eggs
225g (8oz) plain flour
1 tsp bicarbonate of soda
1 tsp baking powder

FOR THE TOFFEE SAUCE

275g (10oz) golden syrup
275g (10oz) light brown sugar
100g (4oz) butter
225ml (8fl oz) cream
½ tsp vanilla extract

If you're the type who can never make up your mind between sticky toffee pudding or a chocolate dessert on a menu, then you will be doubly satisfied with this.

1 Preheat the oven to 180°C (350°F), Gas mark 4. Grease the sides of a 20cm (8in) diameter spring-form tin and line the base with a round disc of greaseproof paper.

2 Put the water in a saucepan, reduce to a simmer and soak the dates in it for 10 minutes. At the same time, melt the chocolate in a bowl sitting over a saucepan of simmering water (also known as a bain marie).

3 Cream the softened butter and sugar in a large bowl until pale and soft. Beat in the eggs one by one and then mix in the melted chocolate. Sift in the flour, bicarbonate of soda and baking powder, then add the dates and the soaking liquid and stir to mix. Pour the mixture into the tin and bake in the oven for 1 hour or until a skewer comes out clean when inserted into the centre. Allow to cool slightly before transferring to a plate.

4 To make the toffee sauce, put all the ingredients into a saucepan on a high heat and boil them for 4–5 minutes, stirring regularly, until they are smooth.

5 To serve, place the cake on a large serving plate (with a rim or a lip around the edge) and pour some of the hot toffee sauce over the top. Serve the remaining sauce in a jug or bowl on the side.

Chocolate

Chocolate is one of the most historically important foods in the world. Countless books have been written extolling the many great virtues of this heavenly delicacy, which has been worshipped for centuries.

The chocolate that we know so well and love with such a passion may date as far back as 1500 BC, when the pre-Columbian Olmec tribe in Mexico is thought to have been the first to cultivate the cocoa tree (*Theobroma cacao*). Many centuries later, the Mayans grew cocoa for the dominant Aztecs, and transformed the beans into a cold, spicy gruel, which became an integral part of their ceremonies and rituals. In the sixteenth century, Montezuma, the last Aztec emperor, reputedly consumed many goblets of the drink before visiting his harem, giving the cocoa bean the reputation for its mighty aphrodisiac qualities and for being a great energy-provider. (Many years later, the infamous Casanova would also use chocolate as part of his seductive repertoire.) Because of these qualities, Aztec women were not allowed to eat chocolate!

When Montezuma served the chocolate drink to Cortés, the Spanish conquistador who came to Mexico searching for gold, it didn't take long for Cortés to realise that the cocoa bean was a valuable commodity. He planted the trees in Trinidad, Haiti and the Ivory Coast, where much of the world's cocoa is still grown today. Cortés was also responsible for transforming cocoa from a cold, spicy drink into something hot and delicious with the addition of sugar, cinnamon and vanilla.

Until the eighteenth century, hot cocoa remained a preserve of royalty and the aristocracy, probably because of the ludicrously high tax it carried. It was sold under a special licence by royal apothecaries, who regarded it as a medicinal ingredient. But things changed in the nineteenth century when the heavy tax on cocoa was greatly reduced. Two famous chocolate connoisseurs – Van Houton of Holland and Rudolf Lindt of Switzerland – both played a great role in developing cocoa from a drink into bars of solid chocolate, similar to the ones we enjoy today.

There are three main kinds of chocolate that we now consume: white, milk and dark (or plain), which are mainly distinguished by their level of cocoa solids.

White chocolate: Some might argue that this is not really chocolate at all because it contains no cocoa solids. It does, however, contain sweetened cocoa butter mixed with milk solids, usually with the addition of vanilla. As cocoa butter is derived from the cocoa bean, it can be argued that real white chocolate is indeed chocolate.

Milk chocolate: As the name suggests, this is chocolate to which whole or skimmed milk powder has been added. It is not often used in cooking because the protein in the added milk can interfere with the texture in baked goods. It contains approximately 20–35 per cent cocoa solids.

Dark chocolate: This is, of course, the connoisseurs' and chefs' choice and contains the highest percentage of cocoa solids. The higher percentage of cocoa solids, the less fat and sugar it contains and therefore the better it will be for you (depending on how much you consume!). Dark chocolate also contains many health-improving attributes, such as antioxidants and stearic acid, which is thought to play a part in lowering LDL cholesterol. It also contains traces of iron, calcium, potassium,

magnesium, vitamins B and E and a substance called phenylethylamine, which is often called the 'love-drug' because it may trigger feelings of being in love.

When it comes to choosing dark chocolate, there are quite a few points to consider, but it is really a matter of personal taste. If you want chocolate with a powerfully rich yet not very sweet flavour for a rich tart or cake, buy a chocolate with 70–80 per cent cocoa solids. If you need a bitter chocolate with hardly any sweetness for a savoury dish, such as a Mexican molé sauce, seek out a bitter chocolate with 80–100 per cent cocoa solids. For a basic, everyday dark chocolate for use in things like chocolate chip cookies and buns, I recommend a chocolate with 55–65 per cent cocoa solids. Anything with less than 55 per cent cocoa solids starts to get very sweet and begins to lose its rich flavour.

Always check the contents on the label, which will tell you not only the percentage of cocoa solids, but also if there are vegetable oils in the chocolate. Vegetable oils are not found in good-quality chocolate – this will contain only real cocoa butter. You can tell a lot about a bar of chocolate when you break it in two. If it is high quality with no vegetable oils and emulsifiers, you will hear a clear 'snap'; if there are lots of hidden nasties, it will not snap sharply.

It is not hard to understand why endorphin-raising chocolate is a symbol of sheer indulgence and decadence, and it is possibly the most evocative comfort food. I can never resist the hot white chocolate at our local farmers' market, made with the best creamy white chocolate, or a slice of rich, nutty and moist chocolate and orange amaretti cake, or even just a square or two of the finest 75 per cent cocoa solids chocolate with an espresso. Whenever I am feeling in need of a boost, something chocolatey never fails to delight!

Chocolate and Rosemary Mousse with Rosemary Shortbread

The flavour of the rosemary-infused chocolate makes for a very surprising but wonderfully intense treat. Serve this mousse with rosemary shortbread to complement this unique and interesting dessert.

1 First make the mousse. Chop the chocolate finely. Put the cream and rosemary into a medium-sized saucepan and heat up to the boil. Turn off the heat and leave to infuse for 5 minutes. Then strain into a bowl, discard the chopped rosemary and rinse out the pan. Place the cream back in the cleaned saucepan and bring back up to the boil, add the chocolate to the cream and stir it around until the chocolate melts in the cream. Whisk in the egg yolks.

2 Whisk the egg whites in a separate, medium-sized bowl until just stiff. Stir a quarter of the egg white into the cream and chocolate mixture and then gently fold in the rest using a metal spoon, being careful not to knock out all the air. Put into little bowls, glasses or cups and leave for an hour or two in the fridge to set.

3 To make the shortbread, preheat the oven to 180°C (350°F), Gas mark 4. Cream the butter in a large bowl until pale yellow and light. Add the sugar, and continue mixing until the mixture is fluffy. Add both flours, the salt and the rosemary and mix until thoroughly combined. The dough will be somewhat soft. Refrigerate it for a few minutes if necessary, so that it is firm enough to roll.

4 Roll out the dough on a floured surface to form a rectangle about 5mm (1/4in) thick. Cut the dough into 4 x 8cm (1 1/2 x 3 1/4in) rectangles, or any other shape you like, and place them about 1cm (1/2in) apart on two baking trays (no need to grease or line). Sprinkle with a little extra sugar, if desired, and bake in the centre of the oven for 12–16 minutes, until they are gold at the edges. Remove from the oven, and transfer to wire racks to cool.

5 Serve each of the individual puddings with one or two biscuits on the side.

SERVES 4–6
AND MAKES 36 BISCUITS
VEGETARIAN

FOR THE CHOCOLATE
AND ROSEMARY MOUSSE
100g (4oz) good-quality
  dark chocolate
100ml (3 1/2fl oz) single cream
1 tbsp chopped fresh
  rosemary
2 eggs, separated

FOR THE ROSEMARY
SHORTBREAD
300g (11oz) butter, at room
  temperature
150g (5oz) caster sugar, plus
  2 tsp for the topping
  (optional)
250g (9oz) flour
75g (3oz) rice flour (available
  at health food shops)
Pinch of salt
2 tbsp finely chopped fresh
  rosemary

White Chocolate Truffles with Cardamom

MAKES ABOUT 25 TRUFFLES
VEGETARIAN
75ml (2½fl oz) single cream
Seeds of 8 large cardamom
 pods, crushed finely
150g (5oz) white chocolate,
 chopped
250g (9oz) icing sugar, sifted

These delicate little truffles absolutely melt in the mouth. They're best lingered over (if you have the willpower) and eaten slowly to appreciate the subtle cardamom flavour.

1 In a small saucepan, bring the cream and the ground cardamom seeds to the boil and then set aside to sit for 2 minutes. Bring back up to the boil, pull off the heat and stir in the chocolate until it has melted. Pour into a shallow dish and leave to cool in the fridge for about an hour.

2 When it has completely set, you can shape the truffles. first put the icing sugar into a bowl. With a teaspoon, scoop out pieces of the chocolate mixture. Roll each one in the palms of your hands to make balls 1–2 cm (½–¾in) in diameter. Drop into the icing sugar and toss so that each truffle is coated. Place on a plate and serve.

Chocolate Cocktail

MAKES 4
VEGETARIAN
50g (2oz) dark chocolate
175ml (6fl oz) vodka

TO SERVE
4 tbsp stock syrup (see
 page 162)
30–60ml (1–2fl oz) brandy
 or whisky
10 cubes of ice
100ml (3½fl oz) softly
 whipped double cream

This is the ultimate in chocolate decadence. Anyone who loves chocolate will be hard pressed not to fall head-over-heels for this cocktail. Serve at the end of a dinner party instead of dessert.

1 Melt the chocolate in a bowl sitting over a saucepan of simmering water, allow to cool slightly and then mix it with the vodka in a jug. Pour into a bottle with a lid or a jam jar and shake well. (You can then keep the chocolate vodka for weeks.)

2 To serve, mix the chocolate vodka with the stock syrup and the brandy or whiskey. Stir with or shake with the ice, strain and pour into four martini glasses. Pour boiling water into a cup or jug and warm up a tablespoon in it. Use the warm spoon to drop a dollop of the whipped cream onto each cocktail. Done in this way, the cream should float nicely on the top.

Classic Dishes

These are the foods that inspire deep nostalgia. They will certainly remind you of a particular time and place and are sometimes considered 'retro'. They also fall into the category of delicious, fail-safe recipes that will never go out of fashion, and for very good reason. With so much attention being paid to new food trends, it's easy to overlook these reliable old friends. Don't forget them! I love them all and make them quite often at home.

French Onion Soup

FOR THE ONION SOUP
50g (2oz) butter
1.25kg (2lb 12oz) onions,
    peeled, halved and
    thinly sliced
Salt and freshly ground
    black pepper
100ml (3½fl oz) dry white
    wine
1.5 litres (2½ pints) vegetable
    stock (or beef or chicken
    stock if not vegetarian)

FOR THE CHEESY CROÛTES
2–3 slices baguette per person,
    sliced 1cm (½in) thick
1 clove of garlic, peeled and
    cut in half
25g (1oz) butter, melted
125g (5oz) Gruyère cheese,
    grated

French onion soup is classic bistro fare, and is still served in many French restaurants today. Cheese-topped croûtes are the traditional accompaniment.

· ❋ ·

1 In a large saucepan or casserole, melt the butter and add the sliced onions, seasoning with salt and pepper. Cook over a low heat for about 45 minutes (even as long as 60 minutes), stirring regularly until the onions are a deep golden brown but not burnt. Add the white wine, turn up the heat to medium and allow the wine to boil, uncovered, until the alcohol evaporates. Add the stock, bring back to a simmer and allow to cook for a further 10 minutes, season and set aside while you make the cheesy croûtes – I usually make these while the onions are cooking.
2 Preheat the grill to high.
3 Arrange the slices of baguette on a baking tray in a single layer. Rub each slice with the cut pieces of garlic and brush with the melted butter. Place under the grill for a few minutes until the bread is golden. Remove from the grill, turn over the baguette slices and cover with the grated cheese. Return to the grill until the cheese is melted and golden. The croûtes will last well for a few days in an airtight container.
4 When you are ready to serve, ladle the soup into warm, deep bowls and float two or three croûtes on the top or serve on the side. Serve immediately.

Variation
To serve this soup in the traditional way, preheat the grill to very hot. If you are serving the soup in its pot, cover the top of the hot soup with the croûtes, scatter over the grated cheese and place under the grill until the cheese is bubbling and golden and serve. Alternatively, if you are serving in individual bowls, divide the soup between warm, deep bowls, place two or three croûtes in each bowl so they are sitting on the top. Cover with the grated cheese and grill until golden and bubbling. Serve immediately.

Baked Plaice with Herb Butter

SERVES 4

4 very fresh plaice, on the
    bone or fillets
Salt and freshly ground
    black pepper

FOR THE HERB BUTTER

75g (3oz) butter
1 heaped tbsp mixed chopped
    fresh herbs, such as parsley,
    fennel, thyme, lemon balm
    and chives
Lemon juice, to taste

TO SERVE

4 wedges of lemon (optional)

Fresh flat fish has been cooked for years at Ballymaloe, simply baked in the oven then drizzled with a herb butter and a squeeze of lemon juice, or served with a hollandaise sauce. All flat fish, including turbot, brill, flounder and lemon sole can be cooked either on the bone (as in the recipe for Dover Sole on pages 93–4), or as lovely rolled-up fillets.

— ❋ —

1 Preheat the oven to 180°C (350°F), Gas mark 4.

2 If you are cooking a whole fish on the bone, follow the preparation and cooking instructions as for Dover Sole on pages 93–4.

3 If you are cooking fillets, pour 60ml (2fl oz) of water into a roasting tin, which will create steam in the oven to cook the fish. Then roll up each fillet from the wide end and place in a dish that is just large enough to contain all the rolled fillets. Lay the fillets with the loose ends facing down. Sprinkle with salt and pepper, cover with foil, stand the container in the roasting tin and bake in the oven for 10–15 minutes. The fish is cooked when the flesh is opaque white with no trace of pink.

4 To make the herb butter, melt the butter in a pan, then add the herbs and a squeeze of lemon juice to taste. Keep warm.

5 When you are ready to serve, remove the cooked fillet rolls from their dish and carefully place on warm serving plates.

6 If you are serving whole fish, remove the cooked fish from the roasting tin, pull the skin from the tail end and peel it off gently. I like to serve it on the bone, but of course you can take it off the bone using a fish slice or palette knife.

7 Pour the hot herb butter over the fish, place a wedge of lemon on the plate, if using, and serve.

Dutch Cheese Croquettes

**MAKES ABOUT 20
CROQUETTES
VEGETARIAN**
225g (8oz) roux (see page 30)
450ml (16fl oz) milk
2 egg yolks
225g (8oz) Cheddar cheese,
  grated
1 heaped tbsp snipped fresh
  chives

FOR THE COATING
100g (4oz) plain flour
Salt and freshly ground black
  pepper
1 egg
Dried breadcrumbs, toasted

These have been made at Ballymaloe for many years (shown with the Baked Plaice on the previous page), and if they do not appear on the Sunday lunch buffet there is uproar! They're crunchy on the outside, with a melting cheesy goodness on the inside ... need I say more? Make them an hour or two in advance of cooking (they will actually be fine for up to two days) and store in the fridge in their coating until it is time to cook them.

1 Pour the milk into a medium-size pan, bring it to the boil and then reduce to a simmer. Whisk in enough roux while the milk is simmering to make a thick white sauce. Then stir in the egg yolks, cheese and chives and leave to cool off the heat. Shape the mixture into about 20 sausage-shaped croquettes or round balls.
2 To prepare the coating, place the flour on a plate and season with salt and pepper. In a bowl, beat the egg. Spread out the breadcrumbs on another plate. Dip each croquette in the seasoned flour, brush with egg and then roll in the toasted breadcrumbs.
3 These are best deep-fried but can be fried in shallow oil. Pour 2cm (3/4in) sunflower oil into a deep, medium-sized saucepan and heat to 160°C (325°F). If the oil is any hotter, the filling tends to leak out in the fryer. To check if the oil is hot enough, drop in a breadcrumb. If it comes back up to the top relatively quickly, the oil is the perfect temperature for frying. If it immediately burns, the oil is too hot.
4 When the oil is at the right temperature, add the croquettes and cook for about 8 minutes, turning over a few times. Drain on kitchen paper and serve immediately.

Smoked Fish Pie with Hard-boiled Eggs

Fish pie is one of those wonderful old-fashioned recipes that will never cease to be a favourite. It tastes all the better with this lovely selection of smoked fish.

———————————— ❊ · ————————————

1 Preheat the oven to 180°C (350°F), Gas mark 4.

2 Place the pieces of fish in a wide sauté pan or frying pan, add the quartered onion and bay leaf and pour over the milk. Bring the milk up to a light boil, reduce the heat and simmer for about 8 minutes until the fish is just cooked. Remove the fish from the milk and place on a plate. Using a fork, flake the fish into nice chunky pieces, then spread out in an ovenproof dish, about 22cm (8¹/₂in) square or smaller individual dishes. Pour the milk through a sieve into a jug and set aside.

3 Cook the potatoes for the mash, as described on page 27.

4 To boil the eggs, bring a small pot of water to a gentle boil, then carefully lower the eggs in and boil for just 8 minutes. Drain and cool the eggs under cold water. Peel the eggs, cut into chunks of about 2cm (³/₄in) and place on top of the fish. Sprinkle with the chopped parsley.

5 Next make the white sauce. Melt the butter in a medium saucepan, stir in the flour and cook for 1 minute over a moderate heat. Gradually add all the fish poaching milk, whisking all the time, and allow to simmer for 1–2 minutes, stirring, until you have a smooth, slightly thick sauce. Remove from the heat, season with salt, pepper and the grated nutmeg, then pour over the fish and eggs in the dish.

6 Arrange the mashed potato over the top of the sauce, score with a fork and sprinkle with the grated cheese. Place in the oven and cook for about 30 minutes, until bubbling and golden on top.

Variations

Seafood: Add 200g (7oz) raw peeled langoustines or prawns to the baking dish along with the poached fish.

Salmon and dill: Replace all of the fish with 700g (1¹/₂lb) skinless salmon fillets, and use dill instead of the parsley.

Fish and vegetable: Add 100g (4oz) each frozen peas and sweetcorn to the baking dish before pouring over the sauce.

SERVES 4–6

350g (12oz) skinned fish, such as ling, hake, cod, haddock or salmon
350g (12oz) undyed smoked haddock, skin removed
1 small onion, peeled and quartered
1 bay leaf
450ml (16fl oz) milk
1kg (2lb 4oz) mashed potatoes (see page 27)
4 eggs
2 tbsp chopped fresh parsley

FOR THE WHITE SAUCE
25g (1oz) butter
25g (1oz) plain flour
Salt and freshly ground black pepper
Pinch of freshly grated nutmeg
50g (2oz) Gruyère or Cheddar cheese, grated

Rachel's handy tips *

* If some of the pieces of fish are from the tail end of the fillet, they will be thinner than the rest of the fillet, so to ensure even cooking, fold the thinner pieces in half to make all the fish more even in size prior to poaching.

* If you want to make this pie for another time, freeze it before cooking in the oven, then thaw and cook as in Step 6, but for about 40 minutes instead of 30 minutes. It will also keep in the fridge overnight.

Mussels with Garlic and Breadcrumbs

This is such a great classic recipe. Serve with some freshly baked bread, such as Dad's Brown Bread on page 38, or little pieces of toast on the side to mop up all the garlicky juices.

—————————— · ✳ · ——————————

1 Check over the mussels and if any are open, give them a tap; if they don't close, discard them. Place the tightly shut mussels in a large saucepan on a low heat with just 1 tablespoon of water and cover with the lid. They will open in the steam. If you catch them when they are just opening, they will be delicious and juicy, so don't overcook them. Remove the mussels from the pan (keeping any juices for a fish soup, pie, stew or even mix with mayonnaise to serve with shellfish like prawns or shrimps). Don't eat any cooked mussels that have not opened.

2 Remove half a shell from each mussel and discard and pull out the beard – the little fibrous tuft – from the straight side of each mussel.

3 Melt the butter in a medium-sized saucepan, add the breadcrumbs, garlic and parsley and mix together. Spoon and pack in quite tightly the garlic crumbs on top of each mussel. Place the mussels, crumb side up, in a single layer on ovenproof plates or gratin dishes (these can be prepared up to 24 hours in advance), and when you are ready to eat, pop them under a preheated grill until golden, crunchy and bubbly.

Variations

Sometimes I feel like adding a bit more zip to this recipe, so in place of the parsley, I add 1 tablespoon chopped coriander together with 1/4–1/2 chopped, deseeded red chilli.

SERVES 4–6

900g (2lb) mussels in their
   shells, scrubbed clean
50g (2oz) butter
50g (2oz) white breadcrumbs
   (see the handy tip on
   page 109)
1 large clove of garlic, peeled
   and crushed or grated
1 tbsp chopped fresh parsley

Roast Loin of Pork Stuffed with Prunes and Apples with a Calvados Sauce

SERVES 4–6

1kg (2lb 4oz) loin of pork
    with skin on (boned and
    ready to roll)
Salt and freshly ground
    black pepper
50g (2oz) caster sugar
1 tbsp ground cinnamon
300g (11oz) stoned prunes,
    finely chopped
300g (11oz) cooking apples,
    peeled and finely chopped

FOR THE CALVADOS SAUCE

50g (2oz) butter
175ml (6fl oz) calvados
250ml (9fl oz) chicken stock
75ml (2¹/2fl oz) single cream

This is an extraordinary recipe that is also an old Ballymaloe favourite. It fills the house with a rustic autumnal aroma while it is roasting, and when you cut through the skin, the cinnamon coats the meat and the warm fruit. The Calvados sauce makes this superb roast something utterly memorable. It would also make a fantastic Christmas dinner in place of traditional turkey.

· ✳ ·

1 Preheat the oven to 190°C (375°), Gas mark 5.

2 Score the skin lengthways at 5mm (¹/4in) intervals, just through the skin, not down to the meat. Then turn it over so that the skin is on the work surface. Season with salt and pepper and evenly dust with the sugar and cinnamon. Mix together the chopped prunes and apples and place in an even layer down the centre of the pork. Roll tightly and tie with undyed cotton twine.

3 Cook in the oven for 1 hour or until the pork is cooked in the centre. To check it is cooked right through, stick a metal skewer into the centre, leave for 30 seconds and if it's then too hot to place on the inside of your wrist, the pork is cooked. If it starts looking a little dark towards the end of its cooking time, cover the joint with foil.

4 To make the sauce, melt the butter in a medium-sized, high-sided saucepan. Add the calvados and allow to boil for 1 minute. Add the chicken stock and boil for 3–4 minutes and then, finally, add the cream and boil for another 2 minutes, or until it has a good flavour. Transfer the sauce into a jug and serve with the sliced pork.

Classic Lasagne with Roast Garlic Bread

SERVES 4–6

FOR THE BOLOGNESE SAUCE
1 small onion, peeled and
    coarsely chopped
1 small carrot, peeled and
    coarsely chopped
1 celery stalk, coarsely
    chopped
15g (½oz) butter
1 tbsp olive oil
2 cloves of garlic, peeled
    and crushed or grated
250g (9oz) minced beef or 125g
    (4½oz) minced beef and
    125g (4½oz) minced pork
75ml (2½fl oz) white wine
75ml (2½fl oz) beef, chicken
    or vegetable stock
1 x 400g tin chopped tomatoes
Salt, freshly ground black
    pepper and sugar
1–2 tbsp chopped fresh basil
1 tbsp chopped fresh parsley

FOR THE BÉCHAMEL SAUCE
50g (2oz) butter
50g (2oz) flour
600ml (1 pint) milk
75g (3oz) grated cheese, such
    as Parmesan or Parmesan
    and Gruyère

12 lasagne sheets
    (approximately 200g/7oz,
    depending on size of dish)

FOR THE ROAST GARLIC BREAD
175g (6oz) butter
6–8 cloves of garlic, peeled
    and crushed or grated
2 tbsp chopped fresh parsley
1 baguette

This may seem quite basic, but this is an essential recipe to add to your repertoire. Not only is it utterly delicious in its own right, but the two sauces are the building blocks for so many other meals. Once you've mastered them, you'll have the basis for many other simple, classic dishes such as spaghetti bolognese or dishes requiring a white sauce.

※

1 Preheat the oven to 180°C (350°F), Gas mark 4.

2 First make the Bolognese sauce. Place the onion, carrot and celery in a food processor and whiz until finely chopped. Put the butter and olive oil in a saucepan on a medium heat and when the butter melts, add the onion, carrot and celery and stir over a medium heat for 3–4 minutes until the vegetables are cooked and light golden.

3 Turn up the heat, add the garlic and beef and stir, breaking up the lumps of mince until it changes colour. Then add the wine, stock and tomatoes (and all their juice) and season with salt, pepper and a good pinch of sugar. Bring to the boil and reduce the heat to low, simmering with the lid off for about 20 minutes until the Bolognese sauce is quite thick. Finally, add the chopped basil and parsley and season to taste.

4 Next make the béchamel sauce. Melt the butter in a medium-sized saucepan, add the flour and cook for 1–2 minutes on a medium heat, stirring so the flour does not burn. Take it off the heat for a moment while you gradually add the milk, whisking all the time. Place the pan back on the heat and whisk until the milk thickens. Season to taste and set aside.

5 To assemble the lasagne, spoon a little Bolognese sauce (about 4 tablespoons), to cover the base of a gratin dish measuring

approximately 25cm (10in) square, then cover with a layer of béchamel sauce and sprinkle with cheese. Place sheets of lasagne in a single layer to cover the cheese, then top with Bolognese sauce and continue until you almost get to the top of the gratin dish. Don't fill it too much, or it will bubble over in the oven – stop about 1cm (1/2in) from the top, finishing with a layer of pasta, then béchamel and finally the cheese.

6 When you are ready to eat, place in the oven for about 30–40 minutes until the pasta is cooked and the top is golden and bubbling around the edges.

7 Meanwhile, prepare the garlic bread. In a small saucepan, melt the butter, then add the garlic and chopped parsley. Cut along the baguette horizontally (or into smaller slices) and generously brush the melted garlic butter over the cut sides. Put on a baking tray and place in the oven for 15 minutes or until toasted and golden brown.

8 Serve the lasagne with the garlic bread and a green salad.

Rachel's handy tips

By putting the lasagne sheets in a dish and covering with boiling water for 2–3 minutes before assembling, the pasta is even more moist when it's cooked.

Chicken Kiev with Sauté Garlic Rosemary Potatoes

This is a recipe you hardly find on menus these days, but it is such a wonderful old standby I couldn't resist including it here. Served with sautéed potatoes, it's nostalgia on a plate in the best possible way.

1 To prepare the chicken breasts, lay them on a chopping board lengthways in front of you. With a sharp knife, slit the chicken breast lengthways, but don't cut completely in half, and open out. Season with salt and pepper.

2 Next make the garlic butter. In a bowl, cream the butter, then add the garlic, herbs and the zest and juice of the lemon. Spread the garlic butter out onto the centre of the opened chicken breasts leaving a margin of 1cm (½ inch) all the way round. Fold the chicken breast back over to resemble their original shape.

3 For the coating, place the flour on a plate, the beaten egg in a bowl and the breadcrumbs on another plate. Toss each breast in the flour, then coat all over with egg and finally roll in the breadcrumbs, making sure all the chicken is covered.

4 Preheat the oven to 200°C (400°F), Gas mark 6.

5 For the sauté potatoes, cut the potatoes into 2cm (¾in) cubes or into 1cm (½in) thick slices and then dry with kitchen paper. Heat the olive oil in a medium-sized frying pan and add the potatoes, season with salt and pepper and cook over a low to medium heat, tossing regularly, for 16–20 minutes, until they are almond golden and crunchy on the outside and soft inside.

6 Toss in the garlic and the chopped herbs and a little bit more olive oil if necessary and cook for a couple more minutes until the garlic

SERVES 4

FOR THE CHICKEN KIEV
4 chicken breasts, skinned
Salt and freshly ground
   black pepper

FOR THE GARLIC BUTTER
100g (4oz) butter, softened
2–4 cloves of garlic, peeled
   and crushed or grated
1 heaped tbsp chopped fresh
   herbs, such as a mixture of
   parsley, chives and tarragon
Finely grated zest and the
   juice of ½ lemon

FOR THE COATING
50g (2oz) flour
1 large egg, beaten
6 tbsp white breadcrumbs

Sunflower oil and butter,
   for frying

FOR THE POTATOES
8 potatoes, peeled
30–60ml (1–2fl oz) olive oil
Sea salt and freshly ground
   black pepper
2 large cloves of garlic, peeled
   and crushed or grated
1–2 tsp finely chopped fresh
   rosemary or thyme

is light golden and the potatoes are cooked. If you want to keep these warm, do not cover them, just sit them in a warm oven.

7 To cook the chicken Kiev, place about 4 tablespoon of oil and 25g (1oz) butter in a shallow frying pan and heat until hot. Add the chicken and cook for about 2 minutes on either side until golden and then transfer to the oven for about 8 minutes until cooked through. Serve with the sauté potatoes.

Rachel's handy tips ✳

✿ If you are short of hob space, the potatoes can be cooked in the oven. Preheat the oven to 200°C (400°F), Gas mark 6. Toss the potatoes with olive oil, salt and pepper in a bowl and spread out in a single layer on a baking tray and cook in the oven for 20–30 minutes until golden and crunchy on the outside and soft inside. Add the garlic and herbs 15 minutes after the potatoes have gone into the oven, toss and continue cooking.

✿ If you have leftover boiled potatoes they sauté beautifully too. Try adding in crushed spices in place of the herbs, such as 1 tsp of ground cumin or coriander.

Pan-grilled Steak with Béarnaise Sauce and Twice-cooked Chips

Steak and chips – need I say more? They are such a pleasing combination, particularly with the classic French béarnaise sauce and a nice glass of red.

· ———————————— · ❋ · ———————————— ·

1 If you have the time, prepare the steaks an hour or two before cooking. If they are sirloin, trim off any excess fat. Place the steaks in a dish and rub both sides with the cut clove of garlic, drizzle with olive oil and sprinkle with freshly cracked black peppercorns. Place a couple of sprigs of rosemary and the garlic under and between the steaks and leave to sit for a bit.

2 Next, prepare your chips. Heat the oil in a deep fat fryer to about 180°C (350°F). If you don't have a deep fat fryer, oven roast the chips, as described on page 229.

3 Peel the potatoes and then cut into skinny or fat chips – just remember they should be consistent in size. If you want potato wedges, then keep the skins on the potatoes and just scrub them very well. Make sure the raw chips are completely dry before they go into the hot oil and don't cook too many at a time. Cook them in the fryer until they are just soft. Remove and drain. Keep to one side and increase the heat to 190°C (375°F) for later.

4 Now make the béarnaise sauce. In a medium-sized saucepan over a medium heat, boil the vinegar, wine, shallot and a pinch of pepper until completely reduced so that just 1 tablespoon of liquid is left in the pan, making sure it does not burn. Add 1 tablespoon of water and take the pan off the heat to cool down almost completely.

5 When it has cooled down so that you can just hold your hands around the outside of the pan, place the pan on a low heat and slowly whisk in the egg yolks and then the butter. As soon as two pieces of butter melt in the sauce, add two more pieces, and it will gradually thicken. Do not let the pan become too hot; if it does, the mixture will scramble. To prevent this happening, keep taking the

SERVES 4

FOR THE PAN-GRILLED STEAK
4 x 175g (6oz) sirloin or fillet
 steaks
1 clove of garlic, peeled and
 cut in half
3 tbsp olive oil
Freshly cracked black pepper
A couple of sprigs of rosemary
Sea salt and freshly ground
 black pepper

FOR THE BÉARNAISE SAUCE
4 tbsp tarragon vinegar
 (see handy tip, page 229),
 or white wine vinegar if you
 don't have tarragon vinegar
4 tbsp dry white wine
2 tsp finely chopped shallot
 (or onion)
2 egg yolks
100g (4oz) butter, cut into
 cubes
1 generous tbsp chopped
 fresh tarragon
1 tsp Dijon mustard

FOR THE CHIPS
Enough oil to fill your deep
 fat fryer (this varies from
 fryer to fryer)
6 potatoes
Salt

pan off and on the heat. If it's in danger of heating up too much, add a tablespoon of water.

6 When all the butter is in, turn off the heat and add the chopped tarragon and the Dijon mustard. If the sauce looks very thin, it may be that you were too cautious and the heat was too low, so increase the heat slightly and continue to whisk until the sauce thickens, it should be almost as thick as mayonnaise.

7 To keep the béarnaise sauce warm, pour it into a heatproof measuring jug. Half-fill a saucepan with hot water from the kettle and place the jug of sauce in the saucepan to keep warm; it will sit quite happily like this for a couple of hours. When the water cools, just put the saucepan on a gentle heat but do not let the water boil too long or the sauce will scramble.

8 When you are ready to eat, place a grill pan or a heavy frying pan on a high heat (or this can be cooked on a barbeque). Allow the pan to get very hot (it may take 10 minutes). Just before the steaks go in the pan, season with sea salt and pepper. Cook on one side to a good deep golden colour (see the timing guidelines, below) before turning just the once.

9 When cooked, place the steaks on a warm plate and allow to rest for a few minutes before serving.

10 While the meat is resting, put the chips back in the fryer and cook until golden and crisp. If for any reason you do have to keep the chips warm in the oven for a few minutes, don't cover them up or they will go soggy. Sprinkle with salt and serve with the steaks and béarnaise straight away.

Approximate times for cooking steak on each side

	Sirloin	Fillet
Blue	30–45 seconds	1 minute
Rare	2 minutes	5 minutes
Medium–rare	3 minutes	6 minutes
Medium	4 minutes	7 minutes
Medium–well done	5 minutes	8 minutes
Well done	6 minutes	9 minutes

Rachel's handy tips ✳

❀ Cooking chips in this way is a very flexible affair as the first round of frying can be done as much as 24 hours in advance. However long you choose to wait, the trick is just to let the chips have long enough to cool down between frying sessions.

❀ When making Béarnaise sauce for the first couple of times be sure to keep a wide bowl of cold water handy so you can plunge the bottom of the pan in to cool it quickly if it gets too hot. Just be careful of the hot steam.

❀ Tarragon vinegar can be bought or it can be made quite easily by placing a couple of whole sprigs of tarragon into a bottle of white wine vinegar and leaving it to infuse for at least a week. Leave the tarragon in the vinegar and keep somewhere cool. It will last for a year easily.

Pavlova with Mango and Crystallised Ginger

SERVES 6–8
VEGETARIAN

FOR THE MERINGUE
3 egg whites
350g (12oz) caster sugar
60ml (2fl oz) hot water
1 tsp white malt or white
    wine vinegar
1 tsp vanilla extract
1 tsp cornflour

FOR THE TOPPING
400ml (14fl oz) double cream
1 mango
50g (2oz) crystallised ginger,
    finely chopped

Here is an impressive yet incredibly easy twist on this reliable favourite. I love the combination of the mango and crystallised ginger, as does my friend Helen, who gave me this recipe. The meringue needs to stay in the oven for a very long time after cooking, so be sure to plan any other cooking you may need to do accordingly.

— · ✳ · —

1 Preheat the oven to 200°C (400°F), Gas mark 6. If using a fan oven, see tip below. Place a sheet of parchment paper on a baking tray.
2 Beat all the meringue ingredients in an electric food mixer or with a hand mixer at a high speed for 5 minutes or until the mixture is stiff. Spread the mixture out on the parchment paper in a circle about 30cm (12in) in diameter and about 3–4cm (1¼–1½in) thick, making a wide, shallow well in the centre (for the cream and fruit to sit in when serving). Place in the oven, then immediately turn it off and leave the meringue to cook slowly for at least 5 hours (or overnight).
3 Carefully transfer the cooked and cooled meringue to a large serving plate. Whip the cream softly and spread over the top of the meringue. Peel the mango with a peeler, then cut the flesh inwards towards the stone into long thin wedges, 5mm (¼in) thick. Lay these on top of the cream, scatter over the chopped ginger and serve the same day.

Rachel's handy tip ✳

If you are making your pavlova in a fan oven, you won't be able to cook the meringue overnight, in which case cook it in the oven preheated to 140°C (275°F), Gas mark 1 for 1¼–1½ hours.

Variations
Pavlova is a wonderful old standby, and is a fantastic blank canvas for so many other fruits, such as passion fruit, pomegranate and fresh berries. Experiment to find other interesting combinations.

Lemon Tart

This timeless recipe was given to me by a friend, Ka, and I adore it. It's really light and creamy, and not quite as heavy and intense as many other lemon tarts, yet still wonderfully fresh and zesty.

· ❈ ·

1 First, make the pastry, which can be done a day in advance of filling and serving. Sieve the flour and salt into a large bowl. Cut the butter into small cubes and rub into the flour until the mixture is like crumbs. Add the sugar and gently mix in with a fork. Drizzle in the egg yolk and lightly stir it into the mixture with a knife until the mixture sticks. If the mixture does not come together, add 1–2 teaspoons of water. Roll out the pastry into a round about 2cm (3/4in) thick, then cover and chill for at least 45 minutes in the fridge.

2 Preheat the oven to 190°C (375°F), Gas mark 5. Grease a 23cm (9in) shallow tart tin with a removable base with a little butter.

3 When you are ready to roll out the pastry, remove it from the fridge. Place the pastry between two sheets of cling film, which should be larger than your tart tin. Using a rolling pin, roll out the pastry until it's about 3mm (1/8in) thick and large enough to line the base and sides of the prepared tin. Make sure to keep it round, if the tin is round, and large enough to line the base and sides of the tin. Remove the top layer of cling film and place the pastry upside down (cling film side facing up) in the tart tin. Press into the edges, cling film still attached and, using your thumb, 'cut' the pastry on the edge of the tin to give a neat finish. Remove the cling film and pop the pastry in the freezer for at least 10 minutes.

4 Next, 'blind bake' the pastry case. Blind baking is a way of partially cooking a pastry case before adding its filling. Line the pastry with greaseproof paper when cold (leaving plenty to come up the sides), fill with baking beans or dried pulses (you can use these over and over), and bake for 15–20 minutes in the oven, until the pastry feels

SERVES 4–6
VEGETARIAN

FOR THE PASTRY
175g (6oz) flour
Pinch of salt
100g (4oz) butter (from the fridge)
25g (1oz) caster sugar
1 egg, divided and the white lightly whisked

FOR THE FILLING
3 eggs
125g (4 1/2oz) granulated sugar
Juice and finely grated zest of 2 lemons
100ml (4fl oz) double cream

TO SERVE
Icing sugar

dry. Remove the paper and beans, brush with a little egg white and return to the oven for 2 minutes. Take out of the oven and put to one side while you prepare the filling.

5 Lower the heat (or heat to this temperature if filling the case the next day) to 120°C (250°F), Gas mark 1/2.

6 To make the filling, place the eggs and sugar in a medium-sized bowl and, using an electric hand mixer, whisk until pale and creamy (about 10 minutes). You can also do this in a food processor. Add the lemon juice and zest and mix for another 5 minutes, then pour in the cream and mix for a further 5 minutes. Carefully pour the filling into the cooked pastry case in the tin, so it does not spill. Return to the oven and bake for 25–35 minutes or until the filling has just set in the centre.

7 Remove from the oven, allow to cool for about 10 minutes before removing the tart from the tin and transferring to a plate or cake stand. When it's cool, dredge icing sugar over the top, and cut into slices to serve.

Rachel's handy tip *

When pouring the filling into the pastry case, it can be easier to do this while the case is actually sitting on a rack in the oven to avoid spilling the mixture.

Index

A

afternoon tea cake, 128
almonds: blueberry and almond
        muffins, 106
    chocolate Amaretti cake, 190
    Greek almond crescents, 135
Amaretti cake, chocolate, 190
apples: apple, banana and strawberry
        smoothie, 102
    blackberry and apple juice, 102
    cranberry and apple juice, 102
    mango and apple juice, 102
    pork chops with apple sauce and
        mustard mash, 48
    roast loin of pork stuffed with prunes
        and apples with a Calvados sauce, 218
Arabian spiced rack of lamb with
    couscous, 180–1
Asian chicken salad, 155
asparagus: heart-shaped toast with
    eggs, asparagus and truffle
    hollandaise sauce, 166
avocados: guacamole, 73
    Korean beef with avocado rice, 158
    smoked chicken and avocado
        sandwiches, 139
    Zac's Aztec soup, 144
Aztec soup, 144

B

bacon and sausage stew with beans, 34
Ballymaloe balloons, 54
bananas: apple, banana and strawberry
    smoothie, 102
    banana and chocolate bread and butter
        pudding, 53
    banana flapjacks, 50
    creamy coconut prawns with spiced
        banana raita, 20
    fruity pancakes, 66
basil: prawn and basil pâté sandwiches, 139
beans, bacon and sausage stew with, 34
béarnaise sauce, 227–9
béchamel sauce, 220–2
beef: burgers with guacamole and crispy
        bacon and cucumber relish, 73
    classic lasagne with roast garlic
        bread, 220–2
    fillet steak with mushroom and brandy
        sauce and tomato fondue, 98
    Korean beef with avocado rice, 158
    miniature steak sandwiches with herb
        mayonnaise and salsa, 82
    pan-grilled steak with béarnaise sauce
        and twice-cooked chips, 226–9
beetroot: salad with beetroot, goat's cheese
    and toasted hazelnuts, 147
beurre blanc, truffle, 176

biscuits: chocolate biscuit cake, 196
    chocolate chip peanut butter cookies, 77
    Greek almond crescents, 135
    little mocha kisses, 186
    oaty shortbread, 130
    polka-dot cookies, 78
    rosemary shortbread, 203
black tea, 132–4
blackberry and apple juice, 102
Bloody Mary shots, oysters with, 170
blue cheese: leek, potato and blue cheese
        soup, 15
    pear and blue cheese sandwiches, 139
blueberries: blueberry and almond
        muffins, 106
    blueberry jam, 124
    raspberry and blueberry sorbet, 162
bolognese sauce, 220–2
brandy: Champagne cocktails, 140
    chocolate cocktail, 204
    mushroom and brandy sauce, 98
bread: banana and chocolate bread and
        butter pudding, 53
    breadcrumbs, 109
    canapés, 82–4
    cheesy croûtes, 208
    cheesy sodabread, 61
    Dad's brown bread, 38
    heart-shaped toast with eggs, asparagus
        and truffle hollandaise sauce, 166
    Joshua's croque monsieur, 70
    roast garlic bread, 220–2
    teatime sandwiches, 138–9
    wholemeal honey bread, 62–3
Brétonne sauce, langoustines with, 88
broccoli with garlic, lemon and
    Parmesan, 118
brownies, stacked chocolate fudge
    squares, 194
bruschetta, mini mushroom, 84
buns, white chocolate, 129
burgers with guacamole and crispy bacon
    and cucumber relish, 73
butter: garlic butter, 223–4
    herb butter, 210
butter beans: Greek lamb, onion and butter
    bean stew, 33
buttermilk: blueberry and almond
        muffins, 106
    cheesy sodabread, 61
    Dad's brown bread, 38
    fruity pancakes, 66

C

cabbage, sautéed buttered, 113
cakes: afternoon tea cake, 128
    chocolate Amaretti cake, 190
    chocolate and hazelnut caramel

        bars, 137
    chocolate biscuit cake, 196
    iced vanilla cup cakes, 127
    white chocolate buns, 129
Calvados sauce, 218
canapés, 82–4
    mini mushroom bruschetta with rocket,
        olives and Parmesan, 84
    miniature steak sandwiches with herb
        mayonnaise and salsa, 82
caramel bars, chocolate and hazelnut, 137
cardamom: white chocolate truffles with
        cardamom, 204
    yoghurt, cardamom and orange panna
        cotta, 161
carpaccio of fish with peppers and fresh
    herbs, 97
carrots: glazed carrots with herbs, 114–15
    Irish stew, 45
caviar, spaghettini with crème fraîche
    and, 85
Champagne, 91
    Champagne cocktails, 140
    Champagne Dover sole with clams and
        julienne of vegetables, 93–4
cheese: baked cheesy pasta, 41
    baked eggs with chorizo, cream and
        cheese, 105
    broccoli with garlic, lemon and
        Parmesan, 118
    cheesy croûtes, 208
    cheesy sodabread, 61
    chicken and Puy lentil salad with
        coriander, 152
    classic lasagne with roast garlic
        bread, 220–2
    Dutch cheese croquettes, 212
    goat's cheese and sundried tomato
        sandwiches, 138
    Italian baked pancakes with cheese and
        tomato, 16
    Joshua's croque monsieur, 70
    leek, potato and blue cheese soup, 15
    mini mushroom bruschetta with rocket,
        olives and Parmesan, 84
    pasta with roasted peppers and
        mozzarella, 23
    pear and blue cheese sandwiches, 139
    salad with beetroot, goat's cheese and
        toasted hazelnuts, 147
    see also mascarpone
chicken: Asian chicken salad, 155
    chicken and Puy lentil salad with
        coriander, 152
    chicken Kiev with sauté garlic rosemary
        potatoes, 223–4
    chicken with lemon and honey, 157
    Lucca's chicken wings with corn on the

cob and sliced peas, 74
Mum's roast chicken with lemon breadcrumb stuffing and gravy, 109
slow roast chicken with lemon and chilli, 116
smoked chicken and avocado sandwiches, 139
tarragon chicken sandwiches, 138
Zac's Aztec soup, 144
chickpeas: Spanish chorizo and chickpea soup, 12
chillies: harissa paste, 180–1
slow roast chicken with lemon and chilli, 116
chips: oven roast chips, 42
twice-cooked chips, 227–9
chocolate, 200–1
banana and chocolate bread and butter pudding, 53
chocolate Amaretti cake, 190
chocolate and hazelnut caramel bars, 137
chocolate and rosemary mousse with rosemary shortbread, 203
chocolate biscuit cake, 196
chocolate chip peanut butter cookies, 77
chocolate cocktail, 204
chocolate sticky toffee pudding, 198
light and fluffy white chocolate mousse, 185
little mocha kisses, 186
stacked chocolate fudge squares with white chocolate and raspberries, 194
torta di cappuccino, 193
white chocolate buns, 129
white chocolate truffles with cardamom, 204
chorizo: baked eggs with chorizo, cream and cheese, 105
Spanish chorizo and chickpea soup, 12
clams: Champagne Dover sole with clams and julienne of vegetables, 93–4
cocktails: Champagne cocktails, 140
chocolate cocktail, 204
pink pomegranate cocktail, 182–3
rhubarb and vodka cocktail, 182–3
coconut milk: crab and prawn coconut soup, 173
creamy coconut prawns with spiced banana raita, 20
coffee: little mocha kisses, 186
torta di cappuccino, 193
Cointreau: afternoon tea cake, 128
condensed milk: chocolate and hazelnut caramel bars, 137
cookies: chocolate chip peanut butter cookies, 77
polka-dot cookies, 78
coriander, chicken and Puy lentil salad with, 152
corn on the cob, Lucca's chicken wings with, 74

courgettes: rigatoni with courgettes, lemon and basil, 19
couscous, Arabian spiced rack of lamb with, 180–1
crab and prawn coconut soup, 173
cranberry and apple juice, 102
crème fraîche, spaghettini with caviar and, 85
croque monsieur, Joshua's, 70
croquettes, Dutch cheese, 212
croûtes, cheesy, 208
cucumber: baked fish with tomato, cucumber and ginger salsa, 150
cucumber relish, 73
oysters with cucumber and ginger salsa, 170
smoked salmon and cucumber sandwiches, 139
squid, cucumber and tomato salad with a black olive and basil vinaigrette, 148
yoghurt and cucumber raita, 119–20
custard: rhubarb and custard tart, 56

D
Dad's brown bread, 38
dark chocolate, 200–1
dates: chocolate sticky toffee pudding, 198
dessert wines, 92
Dover sole with clams and julienne of vegetables, 93–4
dried fruit: afternoon tea cake, 128
drinks: Champagne cocktails, 140
juices, 102
old-fashioned lemonade, 41
pink pomegranate cocktail, 182–3
rhubarb and vodka cocktail, 182–3
tea, 132–4
Dutch cheese croquettes, 212

E
eggs: baked eggs with chorizo, cream and cheese, 105
heart-shaped toast with eggs, asparagus and truffle hollandaise sauce, 166
scrambled eggs and chive sandwiches, 138
smoked fish pie with hard-boiled eggs, 213–14

F
fish: baked fish with tomato, cucumber and ginger salsa, 150
baked plaice with herb butter, 210
carpaccio of fish with peppers and fresh herbs, 97
Champagne Dover sole with clams and julienne of vegetables, 93–4
fish cakes with lemon and pine nuts, 179
sesame goujons of fish with mushy peas and oven roast chips, 42
smoked fish pie with hard-boiled eggs, 213–14

flapjacks, 50
French onion soup, 208
fritters: Ballymaloe balloons, 54
fruit: fresh fruit sorbets, 162
fruity pancakes, 66
fruity flapjacks, 50

G
garlic: broccoli with garlic, lemon and Parmesan, 118
classic lasagne with roast garlic bread, 220–2
garlic butter, 223–4
mussels with garlic and breadcrumbs, 217
Zac's Aztec soup, 144
ginger: oysters with cucumber and ginger salsa, 170
pavlova with mango and crystallised ginger, 230
goat's cheese: goat's cheese and sundried tomato sandwiches, 138
salad with beetroot, goat's cheese and toasted hazelnuts, 147
gravy, 109
Greek almond crescents, 135
Greek lamb, onion and butter bean stew, 33
green tea, 134
guacamole, 73

H
haddock: fish cakes with lemon and pine nuts, 179
ham: Joshua's croque monsieur, 70
harissa paste, 180–1
hazelnuts: chocolate and hazelnut caramel bars, 137
salad with beetroot, goat's cheese and toasted hazelnuts, 147
heart-shaped toast with eggs, asparagus and truffle hollandaise sauce, 166
herb butter, 210
herb mayonnaise, 82
hollandaise sauce, truffle, 166
honey: chicken with lemon and honey, 157
honey roast parsnips with sesame seeds, 118
old-fashioned lemonade, 41
wholemeal honey bread, 62–3

I
iced vanilla cup cakes, 127
Irish stew, 45
Italian baked pancakes with cheese and tomato, 16

J
jam, blueberry, 124
Joshua's croque monsieur, 70
juices: apple, banana and strawberry smoothie, 102
blackberry and apple, 102

cranberry and apple, 102
mango and apple, 102
melon and strawberry, 102
peach and raspberry, 102
raspberry and orange, 102

K
Korean beef with avocado rice, 158

L
lamb: Arabian spiced rack of lamb with
    couscous, 180–1
  Greek lamb, onion and butter bean
    stew, 33
  Irish stew, 45
  slow-cooked lamb shanks with
    piperonata, 24–6
  slow roast spiced lamb with roasted root
    vegetables, 119–21
langoustines: langoustines with Brétonne
    sauce, 88
lasagne with roast garlic bread, 220–2
leek, potato and blue cheese soup, 15
lemon: broccoli with garlic, lemon and
    Parmesan, 118
  chicken with lemon and honey, 157
  fish cakes with lemon and pine nuts, 179
  lemon breadcrumb stuffing, 109
  lemon tart, 233–4
  old-fashioned lemonade, 41
  slow roast chicken with lemon and
    chilli, 116
lentils: chicken and Puy lentil salad with
    coriander, 152
limes: melon and lime sorbet, 162
little mocha kisses, 186
lobster, hot buttered, 87
love potions: pink pomegranate
    cocktail, 182–3
  rhubarb and vodka cocktail, 182–3
Lucca's chicken wings with corn on the cob
    and shelled peas, 74

M
mangoes: mango and apple juice, 102
  pavlova with mango and crystallised
    ginger, 230
mascarpone: rigatoni with courgettes,
    lemon and basil, 19
  torta di cappuccino, 193
mayonnaise, herb, 82
melon: melon and lime sorbet, 162
  melon and strawberry juice, 102
meringues: pavlova with mango and
    crystallised ginger, 230
milk chocolate, 200
mint: tomato, yoghurt and mint sauce, 179
mocha kisses, 186
mousses: chocolate and rosemary mousse
    with rosemary shortbread, 203
  light and fluffy white chocolate
    mousse, 185

muffins, blueberry and almond, 106
mushrooms: fillet steak with mushroom
    and brandy sauce and tomato
    fondue, 98
  mini mushroom bruschetta with rocket,
    olives and Parmesan, 84
  pork and mushroom pie with gentle
    spices, 30
mussels with garlic and breadcrumbs, 217
mutton: Irish stew, 45

O
oats: flapjacks, 50
  oaty shortbread, 130
old-fashioned lemonade, 41
olives: black olive and basil vinaigrette, 148
  mini mushroom bruschetta with rocket,
    olives and Parmesan, 84
onions: French onion soup, 208
  Greek lamb, onion and butter bean
    stew, 33
  Irish stew, 45
oolong tea, 134
oranges: raspberry and orange juice, 102
  yoghurt, cardamom and orange panna
    cotta, 161
oven roast chips, 42
oysters, 169–70
  opening, 169
  oysters with Bloody Mary shots, 170
  oysters with cucumber and ginger
    salsa, 170

P
pancakes: fruity pancakes, 66
  Italian baked pancakes with cheese
    and tomato, 16
panch puran, 20
panna cotta, yoghurt, cardamom and
    orange, 161
parsnips: honey roast parsnips with
    sesame seeds, 118
pasta: baked cheesy pasta, 41
  classic lasagne with roast garlic
    bread, 220–2
  pasta with roasted peppers and
    mozzarella, 23
  rigatoni with courgettes, lemon and
    basil, 19
  spaghettini with caviar and crème
    fraîche, 85
pâté, prawn and basil, 139
pavlova with mango and crystallised
    ginger, 230
peach and raspberry juice, 102
peanut butter: chocolate chip peanut butter
    cookies, 77
pears: pear and blue cheese
    sandwiches, 139
  pear sorbet, 162
peas: Lucca's chicken wings with corn on
    the cob and shelled peas, 74

sesame goujons of fish with mushy peas
    and oven roast chips, 42
peppers: carpaccio of fish with peppers and
    fresh herbs, 97
  pasta with roasted peppers and
    mozzarella, 23
  slow-cooked lamb shanks with
    piperonata, 24–6
pies: pork and mushroom pie with gentle
    spices, 30
  smoked fish pie with hard-boiled
    eggs, 213–14
pine nuts, fish cakes with lemon and, 179
pink pomegranate cocktail, 182–3
pizzas, homemade, 68–70
plaice: baked plaice with herb butter, 210
  sesame goujons of fish with mushy peas
    and oven roast chips, 42
polka-dot cookies, 78
pomegranate cocktail, 182–3
pork: pork and mushroom pie with gentle
    spices, 30
  pork chops with apple sauce and
    mustard mash, 48
  roast loin of pork stuffed with prunes
    and apples with a Calvados sauce, 218
potatoes: chicken Kiev with sauté garlic
    rosemary potatoes, 223–4
  Granny's roast herbed potatoes, 114
  Irish stew, 45
  leek, potato and blue cheese soup, 15
  oven roast chips, 42
  perfect mash, 27
  pork chops with apple sauce and
    mustard mash, 48
  smoked fish pie with hard-boiled
    eggs, 213–14
  twice-cooked chips, 227–9
prawns: crab and prawn coconut soup, 173
  creamy coconut prawns with spiced
    banana raita, 20
  prawn and basil pâté sandwiches, 139
prunes: roast loin of pork stuffed with
    prunes and apples with a Calvados
    sauce, 218

R
raisins: fruity flapjacks, 50
raita: spiced banana, 20
  yoghurt and cucumber, 119–20
raspberries: peach and raspberry juice, 102
  raspberry and blueberry sorbet, 162
  raspberry and orange juice, 102
  stacked chocolate fudge squares with
    white chocolate and raspberries, 194
red wines, 90
relish, cucumber, 73
rhubarb: rhubarb and custard tart, 56
  rhubarb and vodka cocktail, 182–3
rice: Korean beef with avocado rice, 158
rigatoni with courgettes, lemon and
    basil, 19

rocket, mini mushroom bruschetta with, 84
root vegetables: root vegetable mash, 113
    slow roast spiced lamb with roasted root vegetables, 119–21
rosé wines, 91
rosemary: chicken Kiev with sauté garlic rosemary potatoes, 223–4
    chocolate and rosemary mousse with rosemary shortbread, 203

S
salads: Asian chicken salad, 155
    beetroot, goat's cheese and toasted hazelnuts, 147
    chicken and Puy lentil salad with coriander, 152
    squid, cucumber and tomato salad with a black olive and basil vinaigrette, 148
    watercress salad with coriander dressing, 179
salsas: cucumber and ginger, 170
    tomato, 82
    tomato, cucumber and ginger, 150
sandwiches, teatime, 138–9
    goat's cheese and sundried tomatoes, 138
    pear and blue cheese, 139
    prawn and basil pâté, 139
    scrambled eggs and chives, 138
    smoked chicken and avocado, 139
    smoked salmon and cucumber, 139
    tarragon chicken, 138
sauces: apple, 48
    béarnaise, 227–9
    béchamel, 220–2
    bolognese, 220–2
    Brétonne, 88
    Calvados, 218
    gravy, 109
    mushroom and brandy, 98
    toffee, 198
    tomato, 68
    tomato, yoghurt and mint, 179
    white, 213–14
sausages: bacon and sausage stew with beans, 34
scallops with truffle beurre blanc, 176
scones with blueberry jam, 124
seeds, flapjacks with, 50
sesame seeds: honey roast parsnips with sesame seeds, 118
    sesame goujons of fish with mushy peas and oven roast chips, 42
sherry, 91–2
shortbread: oaty shortbread, 130
    rosemary shortbread, 203
Smarties: polka-dot cookies, 78
smoked chicken and avocado sandwiches, 139
smoked haddock: smoked fish pie with hard-boiled eggs, 213–14
smoked salmon and cucumber

sandwiches, 139
smoothie, apple, banana and strawberry, 102
sodabread, cheesy, 61
sole: Champagne Dover sole with clams and julienne of vegetables, 93–4
sorbets: melon and lime, 162
    pear, 162
    raspberry and blueberry, 162
soups: crab and prawn coconut soup, 173
    French onion soup, 208
    leek, potato and blue cheese soup, 15
    Spanish chorizo and chickpea soup, 12
    Zac's Aztec soup, 144
spaghettini with caviar and crème fraîche, 85
Spanish chorizo and chickpea soup, 12
sparkling wines, 91
squid, cucumber and tomato salad with a black olive and basil vinaigrette, 148
steak: cooking times, 228
    fillet steak with mushroom and brandy sauce and tomato fondue, 98
    pan-grilled steak with béarnaise sauce and twice-cooked chips, 227–9
stews: bacon and sausage stew with beans, 34
    Irish stew, 45
sticky toffee pudding, chocolate, 198
stock syrup, 162
strawberries: apple, banana and strawberry smoothie, 102
    melon and strawberry juice, 102
stuffing, lemon breadcrumb, 109
Sunday roast, 108–9
sweet scones with blueberry jam, 124
sweet wines, 92
syrup, stock, 162

T
tarragon chicken sandwiches, 138
tarts: lemon tart, 233–4
    rhubarb and custard tart, 56
tea, 132–4
teatime sandwiches, 138–9
toast, heart-shaped, 166
toffee sauce, 198
tomatoes: bacon and sausage stew with beans, 34
    baked fish with tomato, cucumber and ginger salsa, 150
    classic lasagne with roast garlic bread, 220–2
    fillet steak with mushroom and brandy sauce and tomato fondue, 98
    goat's cheese and sundried tomato sandwiches, 138
    Italian baked pancakes with cheese and tomato, 16
    oysters with Bloody Mary shots, 170
    pasta with roasted peppers and mozzarella, 23

salsa, 82
slow-cooked lamb shanks with piperonata, 24–6
Spanish chorizo and chickpea soup, 12
squid, cucumber and tomato salad with a black olive and basil vinaigrette, 148
tomato sauce, 68
tomato, yoghurt and mint sauce, 179
torta di cappuccino, 193
truffle oil: heart-shaped toast with eggs, asparagus and truffle hollandaise sauce, 166
    pan-fried scallops with truffle beurre blanc, 176
truffles, white chocolate with cardamom, 204
twice-cooked chips, 227–9

V
vegetables: Champagne Dover sole with clams and julienne of vegetables, 93–4
    root vegetable mash, 113
    slow roast spiced lamb with roasted root vegetables, 119–21
vinaigrette, black olive and basil, 148
vodka: chocolate cocktail, 204
    oysters with Bloody Mary shots, 170
    pink pomegranate cocktail, 182–3
    rhubarb and vodka cocktail, 182–3

W
watercress salad with coriander dressing, 179
white chocolate, 200
white chocolate buns, 129
white chocolate truffles with cardamom, 204
white sauce, 213–14
white tea, 134
white wines, 90–1
wholemeal honey bread, 62–3
wine: Champagne cocktails, 140
    choosing, 90–2

Y
yoghurt: tomato, yoghurt and mint sauce, 179
    yoghurt and cucumber raita, 119–21
    yoghurt, cardamom and orange panna cotta, 161

Z
Zac's Aztec soup, 144

Author's acknowledgements

This book would not have happened without the
encouragement, support and expertise from so many
people. A huge thank you to:

Everybody at Collins for their never-ending patience,
enthusiasm and sheer hard work: Jenny Heller, Emma
Callery, Lizzy Gray, Moira Reilly, Fiona Marsh, Kerenza
Swift, Jamie Moore, Nick Ford, Ione Walder – you are
all amazing.

My agents at Limelight Management – Fiona Lindsay,
Mary Bekhait, Alison Lindsay and Melanie Waghorne –
for being there 24 hours a day, and organising my life!

My parents-in-law, Tim and Darina Allen, and to Myrtle
Allen and Hazel Allen for all the help and support and
for allowing us to take photographs and film around
the farm and gardens at the Ballymaloe Cookery School
and Ballymaloe House. Thanks also to Lydia Allen.

David Hare, Brian Walsh, Rory O'Connell, Jimmy
Connolly and the fabulous (as always) TV crew: Trevor
McCallum, Billy Keady, Ray de Brún, Sally Walker, Anna
Ní, Mhaonaigh and Debbie Shaw.

All at Smith and Gilmour, I love your gorgeous designs.

Georgia Glynn Smith, ably assisted by Richard 'Ricardo'
Johnson, for the fab photos and for making the shoot
so much fun, together with Annie Nichols and Róisín
Nield for making the food look so beautiful.

Canice Sharkey and Michael and Katherine Ryan
at Isaac's Restaurant, William and Aisling O'Callaghan
at Longueville House, Justin and Jenny Greene at
Ballyvolane House, Lola O'Conaill at O'Conaill's
Chocolate, Mary Cowman at the Long Point and
Geraldine at Mr Bell's, for kindly allowing us to invade
and film for the television series.

Sharon Hogan, Liz Mullins and Gillian Beamish,
Helen Eck, Dervilla O'Flynn, Grainne Rigney, Michael
Etherington, Linda Shanks, Bill Casey, Sean and Dorothy
Walsh at The Village Greengrocers, Sean McGrath,
Cliffords Butchers and Mary Curran Morrissey at
Castlemartyr Florists.

And finally, a very special thanks to Isaac and all
my precious family in Cork and Dublin, who
continuously support, inspire and mind me, and
keep me relatively sane!

This paperback edition published in 2009 by Collins

First published in 2007 by Collins,
an imprint of HarperCollins Publishers Ltd
77–85 Fulham Palace Road
London W6 8JB

www.harpercollins.co.uk
www.rachelallen.co.uk

Collins is a registered trademark of HarperCollins Publishers Ltd

Text © 2007 Rachel Allen
Photography © 2007 Georgia Glynn Smith

13 12 11 10 09
10 9 8 7 6 5 4 3 2 1

ISBN 978-0-00-728822-9

Editorial Director: Jenny Heller
Senior Editor: Lizzy Gray
Managing Editor: Emma Callery
Design: Smith and Gilmour, London
Photography: Georgia Glynn Smith

Colour reproduction by Colourscan, Singapore
Printed and bound in the UK by Butler, Tanner & Dennis